# POLICY PAPERS

## NUMBER 16

HEZBOLLAH'S VISION OF THE WEST

*MARTIN KRAMER*

THE WASHINGTON INSTITUTE FOR NEAR EAST POLICY
*WASHINGTON, D.C.*

*THE AUTHOR*

Martin Kramer is associate director of the Moshe Dayan Center for Middle Eastern and African Studies at Tel Aviv University. He is the author of *Islam Assembled* (Columbia University Press), and the editor of *Shi'ism, Resistance, and Revolution* (Westview Press). Kramer was a visiting fellow at The Washington Institute in 1987 and is currently a fellow at the Woodrow Wilson International Center for Scholars.

# CONTENTS

# PREFACE

The foreign hostages in Lebanon are living reminders of the challenge posed to the West by Hezbollah, the Iranian-backed movement of fundamentalist Lebanese Shi'ites. The crisis surrounding Israel's apprehension of a Hezbollah cleric in August 1989, known to have taken part in the abduction of at least one American citizen, underlined the reality that the United States and its allies are still held hostage by revolutionary Islam. Nearly a decade after the seizure of the U.S. Embassy in Tehran set an ominous precedent, Muslim extremists have again demonstrated their ability to dominate and manipulate the attention of the American government.

In this study, Martin Kramer ascribes the origin of Hezbollah's hostile vision of the West not only to the policies of Western governments, but to Hezbollah's own ideological and theological tenets. Hezbollah has conducted its operational campaign with a great measure of strategic and tactical savvy. Yet its thinkers understand and represent its struggle as an Islamic war against Infidelity—a war without borders whose aim is to redraw the map of the Middle East and ultimately fashion an Islamic world order.

The United States is the arch-nemesis of this divine plan, the "first root of vice" that dominates "global infidelity" in framing a policy opposed to Islam. In Hezbollah's view, Israel exists to execute American policy, while most of Western Europe is a co-conspirator of the United States. In Hezbollah's polarized vision of the world, even the Soviet Union is suspected of collaborating with the United States against the interests of Islam. Kramer suggests that Hezbollah is even more dependent upon this dichotomous view of the world than its Iranian patrons. Such a vision represents a moral necessity for Hezbollah, without which the movement would lose its compass.

Recent setbacks suffered by Hezbollah have led to some soul-searching in the movement. But Kramer's analysis anticipates not a lincar diminishing of Hezbollah's zeal, but a desperate striving to prevent the "corruption" of the movement, including continued demonstrations of hostility toward the West.

At a moment when optimism again pervades Western speculation about Iran's future, this timely study warns against extending that optimism to Lebanon—a deeply troubled land that is likely to remain an arena of conflict between revolutionary Islam and the West, even if Iran's own zeal wanes.

Barbi Weinberg
President
October 1989

# EXECUTIVE SUMMARY

Hezbollah has sought to impart to Lebanon's Shiʻites a sense of power by emulating the example of revolutionary Iran, seeking purpose and unity through confrontation with the West. This pursuit of confrontation, while guided by strategic considerations, is grounded in Hezbollah's vision of revolutionary Islam as a future great power, holding sway not only in Lebanon but throughout the Middle East.

Hezbollah's vision is as large as Lebanon is small. Given Lebanon's diminutive size, its multi-confessional composition and the positioning on Lebanon's borders of states hostile to Islam, Hezbollah's ideologues do not regard an Islamic Lebanon as a viable proposition now. Only when the wider region undergoes a profound transformation, through the dissipation of Western influence and the elimination of Israel, does Hezbollah believe that Lebanon's Muslims will gain control of their own destinies.

For Hezbollah, the West is essentially one in its hostility toward this vision, which would be realized largely at the West's expense. The United States leads the campaign against Islam, and wields Israel as a weapon against the Muslims.

Britain, France, West Germany and even the Soviet Union, are partners in this American conspiracy. Only the combined forces of Islam can defeat this powerful combination, and Hezbollah's deference to Iran reflects the value attached to Muslim unity in the face of a hegemonic West.

Several developments have initiated a limited debate within Hezbollah. The movement's discourse has been affected by the success of Iraq in the Gulf War, the tightening of Syria's hold on Shi'ite areas in Lebanon, Western steadfastness on the hostage issue and the defensive and offensive initiatives of Israel. These developments have led some in Hezbollah to favor investing their energies in economic and social consolidation, as post-Khomeini Iran seems poised to do.

Yet many in the movement have found new sources of millenarian hope in the Palestinian *intifadah* and the combined Muslim campaign against Christian privilege in Lebanon. Any process of reappraisal within Hezbollah is bound to be an arduous one which the West can encourage only by demonstrating a steady resolve.

# I  INTRODUCTION: THE PARTISANS OF GOD

In the summer of 1989, the mood and intentions of a Lebanese Shi'ite faction known as Hezbollah—the "Party of God"—again preoccupied the West in general and the United States in particular. The aftermath of Israel's seizure of a local Hezbollah leader in south Lebanon, Shaykh Abd al-Karim Ubayd, served as a reminder that the fundamental conflict between the will of revolutionary Islam and the power of the West had not ended. Hezbollah itself needed no reminder. The movement is obsessed with what it regards as its existential struggle against the West for the very survival of Islam. In the West, in contrast, there is an almost perpetual expectation that the cold war with revolutionary Islam is about to end. But each crisis, particularly regarding foreign hostages, reminds the West of something Hezbollah never forgets: there has been no reconciliation.

The summer of 1988 had been a season of anticipation, of wishful hope that the Islamic revolution led by Iran had turned a corner following the Gulf War cease-fire. Some seasoned Iran-watchers even suggested that Iran would curtail or disband Hezbollah by cutting its support for the movement. Others predicted the impending release of Western hostages held in Lebanon. But Iranian leaders continued to patronize Hezbollah, and to view the movement as a proven asset not to be discarded. Despite its Gulf War setback, Iran sought to maintain its hard-won influence in the Arab world through continued support for Hezbollah. There is now little doubt that Hezbollah is here to stay, and that the Perso-Arab linkage, grounded in a shared Shi'ism, will remain a fixed feature of Middle Eastern politics for years to come.

It is easy to lose sight of this truth amid renewed speculation about the imminent moderation of Iranian policy, and about possible changes in Hezbollah's functional relationship with Iran. A preoccupation with pregnant signals and signs is understandable and justifiable as the West attempts to find a way to release the hostages. Yet far too little has been said about the fundamental convictions that inspire not only hostage-holding, but all of Hezbollah's myriad activities and Iran's long-term commitment to Lebanon's Shi'ite community.

There is nothing secret about the spirit of this enterprise. Hezbollah's mission is formulated in clear ideological terms as the defense of Islam against its enemies, whoever and wherever they may be. Islam, in the mind of Hezbollah, is besieged by determined and conspiratorial foes, who act in the interests of "global infidelity" with its seat in the West. There is room for debate among true believers about how the cause should most effectively be served, and how best to combine the essential ingredients of guile and force in changing circumstances. That debate is conducted in secret and still defies full understanding. But the mission of Hezbollah is plain: the steadfast defense and militant propagation of Islam. Not only is Hezbollah here to stay, so too is Hezbollah's revolutionary message that Muslims must work to break the hegemonic power of the West.

Hezbollah is therefore called upon to take an active role in a struggle that extends far beyond Lebanon. Although Hezbollah first seeks to eliminate the last vestiges of Western power and influence in Lebanon, this is only one aspect of a much larger struggle that is aimed at defeating the West and its supposed surrogates and agents throughout the Muslim world. The final outcome of this confrontation cannot be in doubt: the name Hezbollah directly evokes the Koranic promise that, "the Party of God is sure to triumph."

In this context, Hezbollah has played the role of overt vanguard and clandestine strike force. Hezbollah began as a movement of social and political protest, arising from the breakdown of the Lebanese state. It fed upon millenarian expectations among Lebanon's disadvantaged Shi'ites, stirred by Iran's revolution. In order to survive and compete in the Lebanese arena, Hezbollah quickly established an armed militia. To gain international leverage, the movement created a covert branch devoted to the calculated use of terrorism. The three means at its disposal—persuasion, coercion and terror—have been mixed with consummate skill to advance the cause of Islam.

Given the short time span and narrow geographic confines in which Hezbollah has had to operate, the movement has scored some remarkable successes. Hezbollah has earned its reputation not only by employing unique forms of violence, but by rarely missing an opportunity or overplaying its hand. The movement emerged after the June 1982 Israeli invasion of Lebanon when great powers, neighboring states and established Lebanese factions were thrown into disarray. Hezbollah thrived in the vacuum that was created by the frustration and exhaustion of others. Iran provided the catalyst, dispatching highly motivated volunteers to Lebanon's Bekaa Valley in the months that followed the invasion. Although few in number, they trained, indoctrinated and funded local Lebanese Shi'ites, creating the nucleus of Hezbollah. In little more than a year, the movement expanded into Beirut and south Lebanon.

In October 1983, Hezbollah broke the resolve of the American and French governments in a single morning of suicidal attacks against the American and French Multinational Force contingents in Beirut. Then, in cooperation with Iran, Hezbollah intimidated these retreating adversaries in a calculated campaign of hijacking and hostage-taking. That campaign ultimately reached other parts of the Middle East and Western Europe. Simultaneously, Hezbollah launched a low-intensity guerrilla war against Israeli forces in south Lebanon, contributing to Israel's decision to redeploy in a narrow security zone along its border. Hezbollah triumphed repeatedly between 1983 and 1987, gaining new adherents and territorial enclaves, as well as a fearsome reputation that made its name synonymous with terrorism.

The entry in February 1987 of Syrian troops into West Beirut marked the end of the heroic stage in Hezbollah's growth. Until then, Hezbollah had been free to expend its energies confronting Israel, the United States and Western Europe. But as Syria worked to tighten its grip on Lebanon, Hezbollah invested more resources in guarding its freedom of action against the encroachments of Syria and Amal, the Syrian-backed rival Shi'ite movement.

During 1988 and early 1989, this test of wills turned violent. In a series of pitched battles, Amal succeeded in driving Hezbollah from most of its enclaves in south Lebanon. But in subsequent fighting in Beirut's southern suburbs, Hezbollah overwhelmed Amal. Only the intervention of Syria prevented the liquidation of Amal in its few remaining Beirut strongholds. At the end of 1988, Hezbollah launched an offensive against Amal in south Lebanon, ending in the Iranian-brokered agreement of January 30, 1989, that opened the door for Hezbollah's limited return to the south. As a militia, Hezbollah had established its ability to survive, even though the closing of Syria's grip put plain limits on the territorial expansion of the movement.

The cease-fire in the Gulf War also diminished Hezbollah's ability to win new converts from among Lebanon's Shi'ites. As the tide of Islamic revolution receded, it became unlikely that Hezbollah would win adherents who had not joined earlier, when Iran seemed unstoppable. Iran has realized this and now seeks to expand Iranian influence in Lebanon by courting Amal and coaxing Hezbollah into an uneasy alliance with its rival. But despite predictions that the cease-fire in the Gulf would hurt Hezbollah, the movement did not lose the following it had built during years of conscientious recruitment and mobilization. Hezbollah might have ceased to grow, but it did not fold. Doubt did not turn to despair. Its spokesmen even found new cause for optimism. Syria loomed as a future threat, but in the meantime worked to undermine the remnant of Christian privilege in Lebanon that Hezbollah has also sworn to destroy. Hezbollah also drew hope from the Palestinian *intifadah* in the West Bank and Gaza, in which Islam played a prominent role.

It is difficult to speak with certainty about the movement's future prospects, since these depend not only on the proven devotion and resourcefulness of its adherents, but on the resolve of the movement's opponents and the fortunes of Iran's revolution. All that can be said with certainty is that Hezbollah has demonstrated a genius in exploiting shifts in the balance among Lebanon's warring communities, and a talent for maneuvering in the no-man's-land that exists between more powerful outside forces.

Hezbollah has been subjected to two fundamentally contradictory interpretations. Sensationalist journalists have described the movement as an instrument of terror forged by an Iranian conspiracy, drawing upon almost limitless reservoirs of Shi'ite fanaticism. These mythic representations feed upon a deep-rooted Western awe of Islamic violence, dating from the Middle Ages. The other interpretation, partly a reaction to the first, holds that Hezbollah is not much more than a movement for the redress of Lebanese Shi'ite grievances. Its explicitly utopian message of Islamic universalism is dismissed as a guise for the movement's particular Lebanese purposes. Adherents of this interpretation are apt to declare at any moment that the movement is undergoing an accelerated process of Lebanonization or that it has begun to collapse under the weight of internal contradictions.

Both of these interpretations are speculative. Hezbollah preserves its secrets. At times Hezbollah acts with uncompromising zealotry in the name of Islam. At other times it acts with the calibrated pragmatism of a Lebanese militia. On occasion, echoes of the movement's internal debate can be overheard, but the actual process of decision-making remains shrouded in rumor and disinformation. Since too little is known about the social base of Hezbollah, sociological analysis cannot fill the gap.

Nevertheless, the movement has made a tremendous effort to articulate a vision of itself and the world, in its campaign to win a wider following. This overt discourse, emanating from Hezbollah's spokesmen and media, does not encompass the full range of Hezbollah's inner dialogue. But it embodies the essential ethos of the movement, and the common denominator of the many agendas that are subsumed under the rubric of Hezbollah: opposition to the perceived hegemony of the West in the lands of Islam. This hegemony is most evident in Lebanon, but afflicts the lives of Muslims everywhere.

The object of this paper is limited but precise: it is to present Hezbollah's ideology of struggle against the West as it is presented by the movement's leading spokesmen. The approach of this study is not to regard ideology as a precise and infallible guide to Hezbollah's decision-making, but to see it as "a biased representation of the world oriented toward social action. From it are drawn prescriptions of behavior and action, whether individual or collective."[1] While the coin of ideology in the Middle East has been debased by states, for which ideas often serve only to supplement coercion, movements like Hezbollah are heavily dependent upon the influence of ideas. Unlike Iran, Hezbollah cannot draft young Shi'ites into its armed ranks or send them into battle against their will. Ultimately it must be persuasive if it is to succeed.

Therefore, the best minds in Hezbollah devote their talents to the articulation of Hezbollah's vision and the indoctrination of its following. To dismiss Hezbollah's ideology as a rhetorical facade is to prefer the moot speculation that afflicts the popular understanding of Hezbollah. In fact, Hezbollah's spokesmen are highly articulate, and their use of language and metaphor is masterfully calibrated to appeal to the masses and inspire action. They have consistently succeeded on both counts.

Nor is it maintained here that Hezbollah's assumptions about the world are utterly without foundation. The formulations of Hezbollah's leaders often echo distant truths. The West does have political and economic interests in the Middle East that it seeks to preserve; there is a "special

---

[1]Maxime Rodinson, "Nation et Idéologie," in *Encyclopaedia Universalis*, Vol.11 (Paris, 1971).

relationship" between the United States and Israel; and the United States has worked with conservative Arab regimes to contain Islamic revolution. Yet Hezbollah's understanding of these truths and their interrelationships is driven by an inner dialectic; it is a biased representation that strives for consistency through omission and embellishment. The purpose here is to rearticulate Hezbollah's vision faithfully, in the words of its foremost spokesmen.

The evidence in this paper for Hezbollah's positions is gathered from texts that are sometimes overlooked in the rush of events—Hezbollah's manifesto, official statements, interviews, lectures, speeches—all generated within Hezbollah and expressive of Hezbollah's vision of itself and the world. The spokesmen of Hezbollah have been interrogated via these texts, to elicit their own understanding of Hezbollah's mission. Within Hezbollah, there are occasional departures from the ideas regularly propounded by these spokesmen and some of these departures are discussed here. Like all large movements, Hezbollah experiences problems of communication and discipline. But the purpose of this study is to establish Hezbollah's dominant discourse—those ideas that are systematically expounded by the movement's leading spokesmen as authorized doctrine.

No single text generated within Hezbollah can be understood until the dominant discourse has been established. That discourse is the work of a small group of clerics, whose task is to articulate a coherent and consistent doctrine for the masses. On some points this doctrine is elastic, on others it is fairly rigid. When certain ideas are repeated by the movement's leading spokesmen in an almost unanimous manner, they tend to become principles of doctrine. A precise mapping of the influence of the individuals cited here would be difficult, but those who are named and quoted are all individuals who figure in the first ranks of Hezbollah.

No attempt has been made in this paper to provide an accompanying account of Hezbollah's operational history. Its operations against "global infidelity" have been documented by several journalists, students of terrorism and government agencies.[2]   Elsewhere, an account is given of Hezbollah's internal debate over the tactics employed in these operations.[3] The purpose here is to understand this campaign not only as part of an operational strategy—which it undoubtedly is—but as the expression of a set of convictions about the relationship of faith and power in the world. The paper is presented in four parts: a very broad discussion of authority in Hezbollah; an analysis of Hezbollah's vision of an Islamic world order; an account of its presentation of the United States, Israel, Western Europe and the Soviet Union; and reflections on the centrality of ideas in Hezbollah's rise and subsequent development.

---

[2]See the relevant chapters of Robin Wright, *Sacred Rage: The Wrath of Militant Islam* (New York: Simon & Schuster, 1985); Amir Taheri, *Holy Terror: Inside the World of Islamic Terrorism* (London: Adler & Adler, 1987); Xavier Raufer, *La Nébuleuse: Le Terrorisme du Moyen-Orient* (Paris: Fayard, 1987); Maskit Burgin et. al., *Foreign Hostages in Lebanon* (Jaffee Center for Strategic Studies Memorandum No. 25; Tel Aviv, August 1988); and Gilles Delafon, *Beyrouth: Les soldats de l'Islam* (Paris: Stock, 1989). Also useful is the annual *Patterns of Global Terrorism*, published by the U.S. Department of State. The past political and operational responses of the West, also beyond the scope of this paper, have been reported by John Wolcott and David C. Martin, *Best Laid Plans: The Inside Story of America's War Against Terrorism* (New York: Harper & Row, 1988), and Pierre Péan, *La Menace* (Paris: Fayard, 1989).

[3]Martin Kramer, *The Moral Logic of Hizballah*, International Security Studies Program, Woodrow Wilson International Center for Scholars, Working Paper No.84, Washington, November 1987.

## II  FOLLOW THE LEADER: AUTHORITY IN HEZBOLLAH

The question of authority in Hezbollah is often formulated in the West by asking who—in Hezbollah or Iran—is in a position to order the release of Western hostages. The short answer is that no one is. Authority in Hezbollah is not the institutionalized power to order compliance, especially against the will of another believer. It is rather the power to persuade. The tools of persuasion are words formulated in categories of thought defined by Islam; unless one has mastered these words and their meanings, one cannot begin to persuade. Authority is not vested; it is articulated. A more penetrating formulation of the question would be to ask who is best positioned to persuade the movement to move, whether that means convincing hostage-holders to release their hostages, or persuading young men to offer their lives in suicidal assaults.

As partisans of God, Hezbollah's adherents are most readily persuaded by those who can compellingly claim that they speak in the name of God. The discourse of Hezbollah is fundamentally theocratic; its message purports to be the word of God. For true believers, Hezbollah possesses no vision of its own, only a role in God's divine plan. For Hezbollah's adherents, the movement is graced with divine presence. Hezbollah would never interpret itself as outsiders regularly do, as a concentration of temporal power and ideas, grounded in human needs and interests.

But Hezbollah, like other theocratic movements, faces the dilemma of God's continuing silence. God no longer speaks to man. Yet while Islam admits no revelation subsequent to the Prophet Muhammad, it does allow that God inspires and guides mortals. According to some schools of Islam, God guides the Muslim community as a whole; according to others, God selects persons of unsurpassed piety and virtue as agents of divine will. Most Shi'ite schools rest upon the latter assumption, and each Shi'ite is expected to find and follow a learned man who discerns the light of God.

## THE SUPREME JURISCONSULT

The capacity to represent God is understood in Shi'ite Islam within formal categories defined by traditional political theory and law. This theory is complex and is difficult to represent fairly without a thorough exegesis of legal sources. In essence, however, the political theory to which Hezbollah subscribes is the principle of rule by the supreme jurisconsult, the *wali al-faqih*. A jurisconsult, or *faqih*, is an expert in Islamic law—a law revered as divinely inspired. To master the law is to fathom the will of God, as much as any mortal can in the absence—in Shi'ite belief—of the 12 divinely inspired imams who guided believers through the first centuries of Islam. It is the opinion of many in Hezbollah that the authority of the supreme jurisconsult has no theoretical limits. As one of Hezbollah's foremost clerics, Sayyid Hasan Nasrallah, explained in a lecture on the subject:

> The *faqih* is the guardian during the absence [of the twelfth imam], and the extent of his authority is wider than that of any other person. . . . We must obey the *wali al-faqih*; disagreement with him is not permitted. The guardianship of the *faqih* is like the guardianship of the Prophet Muhammad and of the infallible imam. Just as the guardianship of the prophet and the infallible imam is obligatory, so too is the guardianship of the *faqih*. . . .

> His wisdom derives from God and the family of the prophet, and he approaches the divine. . . . When the *wali al-faqih* orders someone to obey and that person disobeys, that is insubordination against the imam. When the *wali al-faqih* orders someone to be obeyed, such obedience is obligatory.[1]

This is the same doctrine advocated by Ayatollah Khomeini in his famous tract on Islamic government, and it is enshrined in the constitution of the Islamic Republic of Iran. The *wali al-faqih* is constitutionally the leader of Iran, a position occupied by Khomeini from the revolution until his death in June 1989. Hezbollah's "open letter" of February 1985, in embracing this theory, thus constituted a pledge of loyalty to Khomeini:

> We are sons of the nation of Hezbollah, whose vanguard God made victorious in Iran, and who reestablished the nucleus of a central Islamic state in the world. We abide by the orders of the sole wise and just command represented by the supreme jurisconsult who meets the necessary qualifications, and who is presently incarnate in the imam and guide, the great Ayatollah Ruhollah al-Musawi al-Khomeini, may his authority be perpetuated—enabler of the revolution of the Muslims and harbinger of their glorious renaissance.[2]

This fealty is graphically demonstrated in the movement's strongholds by the ubiquitous portraits of Khomeini. He appears on the masthead of Hezbollah's weekly newspaper, *al-Ahd,* and his portrait is prominently displayed on every podium and in every demonstration of Hezbollah. Often Khomeini's visage is accompanied by portraits of leading figures in Iranian

---

[1] Lecture by Sayyid Hasan Nasrallah, *al-Ahd* (Beirut), April 24, 1987.

[2] "Nass al-risala al-maftuha allati wajjahaha Hezbollah ila al-mustad'afin fi Lubnan wal-'alam," (Open Letter from Hezbollah to the Disinherited in Lebanon and the World), pamphlet, Beirut, February 16, 1985, p.6.

martyrology, as well as by portraits of living Iranian leaders. There are also portraits of Lebanese Shi'ite martyrs. But the worn visage of Khomeini is the indisputable icon of Hezbollah.

However, Khomeini did not issue direct orders to Hezbollah in the operative sphere. Hezbollah faced the dilemma of interpreting not only God's silence, but Khomeini's. Khomeini did not visit Lebanon to instruct his Lebanese flock of his will. Leading figures in Hezbollah who visited Khomeini in Iran often found his will difficult to fathom. This is also why the death of Khomeini has not produced a crisis of authority in Hezbollah. Many in Hezbollah would have preferred that Khomeini be succeeded by Ayatollah Husayn Ali Montazeri, who did take a keen interest in the affairs of Lebanon, and who was popular among the Lebanese Shi'ite students in the religious academies of Qom in Iran. But Khomeini's decision to deny Montazeri succession was unequivocal, and Hezbollah has extended its unqualified allegiance to the successor chosen by Iran's Assembly of Experts, Ayatollah Ali Khamene'i.[3] In practical terms, the succession has had no impact upon Hezbollah. Khomeini always remained remote from the affairs of Lebanon, which he delegated to others, and Khamene'i has followed his precedent.

Instead, the adherents of Hezbollah, as well as Iranian emissaries, have been left to arrive at a program of action through mutual consultation and persuasion. During the past several years, these emissaries arrived in Lebanon under a variety of auspices: the Revolutionary Guard, the Foreign Ministry, the Martyrs' Foundation, the Ministry of Islamic Guidance, the Ministry of Intelligence and Internal Security, and leading Iranian clerics have all been represented in Lebanon.[4] The most famous of these emissaries was Ali Akbar

---

[3]Hezbollah's cable of support for Khamene'i, Voice of the Oppressed (clandestine), June 7, 1989.

[4]For Iran's role in the creation of Lebanon's Hezbollah and the movement's growth, see R.K. Ramazani, *Revolutionary Iran: Challenge and Response in the Middle East* (Baltimore: Johns Hopkins University Press, 1986), pp.175-95; Shimon Shapira, "The Origins of Hizballah," *The Jerusalem Quarterly*, No.46 (Spring 1988), pp.115-130; and Martin Kramer's essays in the annual *Middle East Contemporary Survey*, Vol.8 (1983-84),

Mohtashemi, former Iranian ambassador to Damascus from 1982 to 1985, who built much of the logistical base of the movement. His role did not go unnoticed by Hezbollah's adversaries: while ambassador, he was the victim of a letter-bomb attack that took off two of his fingers. Later, as Iran's minister of Interior, Mohtashemi continued to defend Hezbollah's cause in Iranian decision-making circles, where his missing fingers undoubtedly bore symbolic witness to the sacrifices already made for the cause of Islam in Lebanon. It is not certain that his recent removal from the cabinet by President Rafsanjani will silence Mohtashemi, whose revolutionary credentials are impeccable.[5] But Hezbollah was not the creation of Mohtashemi alone, and representatives of all the principal Iranian power centers have played a role in the movement's gestation and growth.

These emissaries brought together the movement's own thinkers and commanders to form a governing consultative council (*shura*). Members of this council meet periodically to consider high policy in consultation with official Iranian representatives. Little is known about the deliberations of the council, which meets in secret. It is only recently that Hezbollah's publications have made explicit reference to the council, by identifying certain persons as members. But the council's very title suggests that, despite the absolute authority accorded to the *wali al-faqih*, consultation is one of the central values of Hezbollah. This emphasis on consultation also serves a functional purpose, since most of Iran's emissaries know little about Lebanon and rely extensively on the judgment of their Lebanese clients, even as those clients profess allegiance to their patrons.

The presence of Iran's emissaries, in mosques, at training bases, on official missions and in the consultative council has cultivated a sense of partnership between Iran and Hezbollah. The dependence of Hezbollah on Iran thus differs in character

---

pp.171-173; Vol.9 (1984-85), pp.155-159; Vol.10 (1986), pp.139-144; Vol.11 (1987), pp.165-169; and the forthcoming Vol.12 (1988).

[5]For a profile of Mohtashemi, see *The New York Times*, August 27, 1989.

from the dependence of other Lebanese factions on outside support. Hezbollah and Iran are bound not only by a coincidence of interests, but by a shared religious ethos and vision of the future, tailored to Lebanese realities in daily contacts between Iranians and Lebanese.

## THE MYSTIQUE OF THE ULAMA

Hezbollah's adherents are devoted to implementing God's law, and therefore submit to the authority of those who are experts in the law. These are the *ulama*, or the clergy, and more particularly the *fuqaha*, or the Muslim jurisconsults who are learned in the law. The *wali al-faqih*, the supreme jurisconsult, offers guidance only in broad matters of principle and has left a wide range of decisions to the discretion of the lesser *ulama* of Lebanon.

Like Islamic Iran, Hezbollah revolves around Shi'ite *ulama*. Their guidance is not merely spiritual, for they would be the first to deny any separation between their spiritual and political messages. They have transmitted to Hezbollah its guiding themes, its millenarian hope, its vision of the West and its justifications for violence. The relationship of the cleric to the layman in Shi'ite Islam evokes that of the master to his disciple, of the initiated to the novice. Bonds of moral dependence link many of the lay activists in Hezbollah to the prominent *ulama* of the movement.

Hezbollah originated among these Shi'ite men of religion, in the circles of their acolytes. Now the movement is so large that contact between the leading *ulama* and the rank-and-file is mediated by lesser clerics, functionaries and Hezbollah's mass media, which include pamphlets, journals, a newspaper and a broadcast station. When Hezbollah's partisans want an authoritative interpretation of where their movement stands, they turn expectantly to the *ulama*.

Authority among the *ulama* is exercised in informal ways, but there is an order of deference. Juniors usually defer to their seniors; the less learned defer to the more learned. These established patterns of deference and submission have been subsumed by Hezbollah without significant modification. Yet there is a large amount of latitude for differing interpretations of the Islamic code, by which all of Hezbollah's actions must be justified. Perhaps the most important differences are rooted in the various backgrounds of the *ulama*.

Many of Hezbollah's clerics preached the doctrine of an Islamic state long before the Iranian revolution. They do not regard themselves as intellectually indebted to that revolution, although they made obeisance to Khomeini while he lived, and are quick to acknowledge the importance of Iranian advice and assistance. This independence of spirit is particularly evident among those Shi'ite clerics who were educated in the Shi'ite shrine cities of Iraq rather than in Iran. Schooled in the strongest Shi'ite traditions by great Arab teachers, they tend to be reserved about Iran's present claim to absolute primacy in the Shi'ite world.

This autonomous faction is led by Ayatollah Sayyid Muhammad Husayn Fadlallah, who is unquestionably the most articulate and subtle advocate of the Islamic cause in Lebanon. Fadlallah was actually born in Iraq, where his Lebanese father was a student and teacher, and he only settled in Lebanon on the completion of his religious studies. From a purely intellectual point of view, Fadlallah owes little to Iran or Khomeini, and he has maintained a steadfast independence, even as he preaches a similar message.[6]

Fadlallah has often been tagged by the press as the spiritual leader of Hezbollah. He denies this, although he is quick to claim that many who are adherents of Hezbollah are also his followers. But Fadlallah has no interest in being singled out as Hezbollah's leader, spiritual or otherwise. Because his ability to persuade is not unlimited, he sees no reason to bear the burden of responsibility for actions which he advised against taking.

---

[6]For biographical details, see Martin Kramer, "Muhammad Husayn Fadlallâh," *Orient* (Opladen, West Germany), Vol.26, No.2 (June 1985), pp.147-149. Aspects of Fadlallah's political philosophy, as revealed in his earliest (and most obtuse) writings, are discussed by Olivier Carré, "Quelques mots-clefs de Muhammad Husayn Fadlallâh," *Revue française de science politique* (Paris), Vol.37, No.4 (August 1987), pp.478-501; *idem,* "La 'révolution islamique' selon Muhammad Husayn Fadlallâh," *Orient* (Opladen, West Germany), Vol.29, No.1 (March 1988), pp.68-84.

But he does have more power to persuade than any cleric openly identified with Hezbollah, and his brilliant Arabic oratory casts a spell on young Shi'ite university students and intellectuals. No other cleric has quite the same effect, and Iran's emissaries are firmly of the opinion that Hezbollah cannot do without him. Fadlallah is intensely egotistical, knows that he is indispensable and openly asserts his moral independence. "I am not an agent for anybody's policy," he insists when asked about his ties to Iran. "I am simply trying to implement my policy, which is based on Islam and which complements all the Islamic world's forces."[7] In fact, Fadlallah has long relied upon the friendship of Ali Akbar Hashemi-Rafsanjani, Iran's new president, with whom he shares an enhanced capacity for guile and dissimulation.

Fadlallah might best be described as the most outspoken and visible of Hezbollah's inspirational guides, instead of as its leader. Although his influence over his acolytes is considerable, it is negligible among many in Hezbollah who look and find guidance from other sources. For this reason, Fadlallah's stated views cannot always be regarded as representative of Hezbollah's positions. In many instances, he is in accord with those clerics who openly identify with Hezbollah; in other instances, he is not. On most points of difference, Fadlallah's views are less doctrinaire and reflect the caution of an older and shrewder man, more experienced in Lebanon's ways and Lebanon's limits than the young clerics who breathe fire when they speak for Hezbollah. Fadlallah's views are representative of the movement only when it can be established that Hezbollah's other spokesmen repeat and embellish his ideas.

A larger group of clerics is much more closely attuned to the requirements of Iranian emissaries in Lebanon. This camp draws its support from relatively recent converts to the cause, who got religion only after Iran made Islam a slogan of revolution. These enthusiasts were brought directly into Hezbollah by the Iranian clerics, diplomats and Revolutionary Guards who have been active in Lebanon since 1982. While

---

[7]Interview with Fadlallah, *Le Quotidien de Paris*, September 23, 1986.

Fadlallah and his close adherents regard themselves as full and equal partners of the Iranians, the converts are encouraged to see themselves as simple soldiers. "Our relationship to the Islamic revolution [in Iran] is one of a junior to a senior," said a leading cleric in this camp, "of a soldier to his commander."[8]

The Shi'ite clerics who are prominent in this group are young, and most received some education in Iran. Among them are Sayyid Ibrahim al-Amin, Sayyid Hasan Nasrallah and Shaykh Zuhayr Kanj in Beirut, and two preachers in the Bekaa Valley, Shaykh Subhi al-Tufayli and Sayyid Abbas al-Musawi. Husayn al-Musawi, the lay leader of Islamic Amal, the Baalbek-based militia, is also identified with this group.

Hezbollah's leadership has demonstrated a unity of ranks that is rare in Lebanon. Despite a considerable amount of pressure brought to bear upon Hezbollah, the movement has not experienced a split. In recent years, the rival Shi'ite movement Amal has undergone repeated splits, its factions have engaged in armed clashes and its leaders have repeatedly maligned one another. Not only has Hezbollah remained united, but the differences that do exist have not been thrashed out in public. The bonds of collegiality among Hezbollah's *ulama* appear to have a moderating effect on their political and generational differences, much as these bonds do within the clerical elite in Iran. The *ulama* appear to recognize that if infighting became public, it would undermine their collective prestige and mystique. There has never been a recorded instance of explicit public criticism leveled by one cleric against another in Hezbollah.

The fact that members of the *ulama* hold no official titles in the movement also prevents clashes over the precise translation of informal authority into bureaucratized structure, in clear contrast to Amal. The clerics of Hezbollah refuse to acknowledge that their authority is structured. Ibrahim al-Amin maintains that the movement is "not a regimented party, in the common sense," because the idea of an exclusive

---

[8]Interview with Shaykh Subhi al-Tufayli, *Ettela'at* (Tehran), August 20, 1985.

"party" is foreign to Islam. Hezbollah is a "mission" and a "way of life."[9] Husayn al-Musawi has insisted that Hezbollah "is not an organization," since its members carry no membership cards and its leaders occupy no formal office. It is a "nation" of all people who believe in the struggle against injustice, and all who are loyal to the person and vision of Khomeini.[10] None of the clerics hold an official title and they disclaim even informal designations as leaders since Khomeini was regarded as "the leader" (al-qa'id)—in imitation of the Persian designation of Khomeini as the "leader" (rahbar) of the Islamic revolution. The refusal to formalize structure has spared Hezbollah the backbiting that always accompanies a jostling for office.

## HEZBOLLAH'S STRONGMEN

Members of the Shi'ite ulama believe in the power of their ideas and words. "I believe that everything can be solved by dialogue," says Fadlallah. "This is the best method. I believe that in all cases violence is like a surgical operation that the doctor should only resort to after he has exhausted all other methods."[11] But when dialogue fails, as it so often does in Lebanon, Hezbollah draws upon its militia and covert branch. The task of the militia is to persuade through the power of arms. The task of those in the covert branch is to persuade through disavowable deeds of terror.

Hezbollah's name appears only on the political statements of the movement. It is never used to claim credit for any military operation or violent act. The Islamic Resistance attaches its name exclusively to guerrilla operations against Israel and the Israel-backed South Lebanon Army. It operates

---

[9]Interview with Ibrahim al-Amin, al-Harakat al-Islamiyya fi Lubnan (Beirut, 1984), pp.145-146.

[10]Interview with Husayn al-Musawi, al-Nahar al-arabi wal-duwali (Beirut), June 10-16, 1985.

[11]Interview with Fadlallah, Monday Morning (Beirut), October 15-21, 1984.

under the nominal command of Sayyid Abbas al-Musawi, with the assistance of lesser clerics such as the now celebrated Shaykh Abd al-Karim Ubayd. Its rank-and-file tends to be drawn from the villages of south Lebanon and the southern Bekaa Valley, and its ethos combines Islam with strong local patriotism.

Islamic Jihad, Islamic Jihad for the Liberation of Palestine, the Revolutionary Justice Organization and the Oppressed of the Earth are names which are used exclusively to claim credit for violent acts such as bombings and kidnappings, directed mostly against Western targets. Hezbollah does not want to be held directly accountable for such acts, even when they serve the aims of the larger movement. But Hezbollah's clerics do provide moral justifications for these deeds, thereby relieving the covert branch of the need to do so. These groups are based in Beirut's southern suburbs and draw from the urbanized poor.

Recruitment is grounded partly in the ideological indoctrination offered by the clerics of Hezbollah. They preach tirelessly at mosques, rallies, funerals—wherever a crowd can be found. But the movement uses many different means to bring followers to its flag. Some of the strongmen in Hezbollah began in the various armed Palestinian organizations that employed Lebanese Shi'ites prior to Israel's 1982 invasion. Many of the Shi'ites who shared the same camps and slums as the Palestinians viewed the Lebanese state with a shared contempt. After the Palestinian collapse in 1982, many of these Shi'ite fighters, who had no marketable skills other than their mastery of light arms, were recruited by Hezbollah, which paid them the best salaries offered by any Lebanese militia. The ideological indoctrination of these recruits was haphazard and they have continued to live lives of controlled banditry. The most notorious of these strongmen is Imad Mughniyya, named by various intelligence sources as the central figure behind many acts of kidnapping, hijacking and bombing.[12]

---

[12]For the most recent theories regarding the composition of the covert branch, and some details on Mughniyya, see the article by Israeli journalist Ehud Yaari in *The Wall Street Journal,* August 16, 1989. See also Brian Michael Jenkins and Robin Wright, "The Kidnappings in

Recruitment also has been accomplished through the traditional Lebanese structures of clan, village and neighborhood. In some areas of the Bekaa Valley, where allegiance is given first to clans (*asha'ir*), it is common for a clan to join Hezbollah *en masse* and thereby serve its collective material interests. "We are opposed to the feudal and clan structure," says Husayn al-Musawi. "But we are not opposed to individuals who are members of these clans. If a clan or family is attacked, it is our duty to defend it."[13] It is largely for the benefit of such clans that Iran has administered an extensive "reconstruction" program in the Bekaa Valley, which includes the renovation of damaged homes, road paving and repairs, the drilling of wells, the construction of reservoirs and the financing of agricultural cooperatives.[14] These benefits, which are offered to entire clans, have won a large following for Hezbollah in a backward region that did not receive basic services from the central Lebanese government even in the best of times. It is in this region that Hezbollah maintains its logistical and training bases, in and around the town of Baalbek. Here, too, is a large contingent of Iranian Revolutionary Guards who do not fight but function in an advisory capacity.

Beirut's southern suburbs—in fact, urban slums—are inhabited by populations drawn from the Bekaa Valley and south Lebanon, and it is common for certain neighborhoods to be identified completely as enclaves of Hezbollah. These neighborhoods, which have become a major recruiting ground for Hezbollah, enjoy a wide range of services offered through the offices of the Iranian-sponsored Martyrs' Foundation. The families of militiamen who are killed or

---

Lebanon," *TVI Report*, Vol.7, No.4 (1987), pp. 2-13 (with comment by As'ad Abu Khalil).

[13]Interview with Husayn al-Musawi, *Nouveau Magazine* (Beirut), July 23, 1988.

[14]Description of activities of the Reconstruction Jihad, *al-Ahd*, August 5, 1988; report on aid to the western Bekaa Valley, *al-Ahd*, February 17, 1989.

wounded in service are guaranteed pensions by the Lebanese branch of the Martyrs' Foundation, as well as other services such as subsidized pharmaceuticals, hospital care and schoolbooks.[15] Recently Hezbollah has begun to establish block committees to look after the needs of individual streets in the southern suburbs.

From the outset, Hezbollah also sought a following within the ranks of Amal, which had commanded the allegiance of the great majority of Lebanese Shi'ites prior to Hezbollah's appearance. Hezbollah demonstrated a certain pragmatism by allowing many of these recruits to remain in Amal. "Believers in the Amal movement fight shoulder-to-shoulder in south Lebanon with Hezbollah brothers against Zionist forces, and there is always mutual understanding between us," said one of Hezbollah's spokesmen at the height of Hezbollah's penetration of Amal. "Our political differences are with the high officials of the Amal movement, not with its lower ranks."[16]

Hezbollah did not encourage the defection of its sympathizers from Amal because it realized how difficult it would be for many of them to make a clean break. Instead, Hezbollah urged these sympathizers to remain in Amal and work to transform the rival movement from within. But intensified violence between Hezbollah and Amal put an end to the fundamentalist penetration of Amal—not because Hezbollah called on its followers to defect, but because Amal's leaders finally decided to purge the movement of compromised elements. A wing of Amal known as the Believing Resistance, under the direction of the disaffected Amal commander Mustasfa Dirani, has come under strong Iranian influence, having been expelled by Amal. But the present effort of Iran to broker an alliance between Hezbollah and Amal is based on the assumption that the transformation

---

[15]The social services provided to members of Hezbollah are described in an interview with the general director of the Beirut office of the Martyrs' Foundation, *al-Ahd*, January 23, 1987.

[16]Interview with Husayn al-Musawi, *Kayhan*, February 9, 1986. Musawi spoke of the "dedicated and pious" members of Amal, whom he considered "part of the Hezbollah movement"; *Kayhan*, July 27, 1986.

of Amal from below has reached its limits, and that it is essential to win over Amal's leaders in order to broaden Iran's influence.

In short, although Hezbollah is a movement that seeks to transform consciousness, it has always been prepared to build upon the primordial loyalties that bind its potential constituencies. Hezbollah will establish any tie, by any means, with potential recruits, especially by offering material advantages in a Lebanon that has been wrenched by economic crisis. Western diplomatic and intelligence sources estimate that Iran's material aid to Hezbollah is nearly $100 million per year, a massive amount of money for a movement that appeals to a disadvantaged confessional community struggling under the weight of a collapsing economy. Indoctrination, the imparting of Hezbollah's comprehensive vision of the world, is often accomplished only after affiliation is established.

The willingness to build on primordial loyalties and use economic leverage has allowed Hezbollah to build a mass following. The principal disadvantage of this kind of recruitment has been that Hezbollah is affected by sources of factionalism that are endemic to Lebanon's Shi'ite community. Without prior indoctrination, it is not always possible to negate the effects of old loyalties. And the many who answered to Hezbollah's material inducements cannot be considered absolutely reliable. Many such ties are tenuous, a fact that has inspired a great deal of speculation as to how Hezbollah functions, and especially whether or not Iran commands and controls every remote cell in the covert branch. One of Hezbollah's spokesmen has complained that "organizations spring up like mushrooms, issue statements, take hostages and do other things. . . . The fact that there are 50 organizations which claim to be serving Muslims, but which are not cooperating with one another in any way, is inexcusable."[17]

It is impossible to know for certain how much leverage Hezbollah's clerics and Iran have at any moment, and even they may not know, since they have never had cause to bring all their persuasive force to bear on all the remote redoubts of

---

[17]Interview with Husayn al-Musawi, *Kayhan*, July 29, 1986.

the movement. Yet all evidence indicates that Iran's legally constituted leaders have never failed to bring about the release of a hostage when they have chosen to do so, even when hostages have been held by close-knit and secretive cells. These cells enjoy considerable latitude in the day-to-day running of their affairs. But if they were to act without the sanction of clerics, they would soon dissipate into renegade gangs. Their task of hostage-holding does serve many private, material and family needs, but can only be sustained so long as it also serves the interest of Islam. "The kidnappers' conditions are Iran's conditions," Husayn al-Musawi once declared, "because they are loyal to the Islamic republic. There is no difference between the demands of individuals and the demands of states. There is a public Islamic interest."[18]

The right of Hezbollah's clerics and Iran's emissaries to define that interest is still beyond challenge. It is Hezbollah that provides the moral justifications, the material means, the sympathetic environment and the negotiating channels which together make prolonged hostage-holding possible. And it is only Iran that can provide protection from Syria, safe refuge for hostage-holders whose lives are endangered and an eventual exit from hostage-holding. The threatened withdrawal of sanction is a powerful tool in the hands of Iran and Hezbollah's clerics. It has been used sparingly, but always with great effectiveness.

To diminish the effects of primordial loyalties, Hezbollah's clerics relentlessly inculcate the message that the movement was created to serve. Once potential adherents become affiliated with Hezbollah, vast energies are invested in imparting to them a vision that is clear, compelling and worthy of self-sacrifice. Followers find their way to Hezbollah along many different paths. What is essential for the cohesion of the movement is that they converge upon a single road and march together toward the realization of God's divine plan.

---

[18]Interview with Husayn al-Musawi, *al-Majallah* (London), April 8-14, 1987.

# III THE DIVINE PLAN: AN ISLAMIC WORLD ORDER

Hezbollah's understanding of its role in the world is rooted in the way it sees its role in historical and contemporary Islam. At the most fundamental level, Hezbollah sees itself not as a Lebanese confessional faction, but as the continuation of a movement created by divine will through the Prophet Muhammad and driven forward through divine history toward the creation of one united world of Islam. Most recently, the instrument of God's will has been the Imam Khomeini, whose success in bringing about an Islamic revolution represented a first step toward the restoration of Islam to its place of primacy. Hezbollah itself is a secondary instrument of divine will, created to spread the message of Islamic revolution beyond the geographic confines of Iran.

## THE DENIAL OF LEBANON

By its own definition, Hezbollah cannot be a Lebanese movement. Its slogan declares it to be the Islamic movement in Lebanon, not of Lebanon. Hezbollah carries out decisions issued by the supreme jurisconsult, whose seat of authority, while distant from Lebanon, is not limited by any border. As Ibrahim al-Amin emphasizes, it is the geography of Islam and not of Lebanon that defines the arena of Hezbollah's activity:

"We do not derive our political decision-making from anyone but the jurisconsult. The jurisconsult is not defined by geography but by Islamic law."

Therefore, no barriers separate the faithful in Lebanon from the faithful in Iran: "We in Lebanon do not consider ourselves as separate from the revolution in Iran, especially on the question of Jerusalem. We consider ourselves, and pray to God that we will become, part of the army which the Imam wishes to create in order to liberate Jerusalem. We obey his orders because we do not believe in geography but in change." As Ibrahim al-Amin declared, "God willing, we will live up to our allegiance to the Imam."[1]

If the authority of the supreme jurisconsult has no limit, then any frontier that artificially impedes the exercise of that authority is illegitimate. Hezbollah therefore operates in Lebanon only as a branch of a larger Hezbollah. That larger movement is composed of all who struggle under the inspiration of Khomeini's vision against the enemies of Islam. According to Husayn al-Musawi, the aspirations of Hezbollah in Lebanon are "an extension of the aspirations of adherents of Hezbollah throughout the Islamic world. . . . Some say we are Muslim Lebanese. No! We are Muslims of the world and we have close links with other Muslims of the world."[2]

Shaykh Subhi al-Tufayli concurs, saying that "We do not work or think within the borders of Lebanon, this little geometric box, which is one of the legacies of imperialism. Rather, we seek to defend Muslims throughout the world."[3] And according to Abbas al-Musawi, "We are all brothers and fighting for the same cause. Any attempt to separate us from our Iranian brothers or from Muslims in general is a crime."[4]

---

[1]Interview with Ibrahim al-Amin, *al-Harakat al-Islamiyya fi Lubnan*, pp. 150-151.

[2]Interview with Husayn al-Musawi, *Kayhan*, July 27 and 29, 1986.

[3]Speech by Shaykh Subhi al-Tufayli, *al-Ahd*, April 10, 1987.

[4]Interview with Abbas al-Musawi, *La Revue du Liban* (Beirut), July 27-August 3, 1985.

Allegiance to Lebanon cannot be reconciled with the vision of Hezbollah; the country's turmoil is the inevitable consequence of its illegitimate genesis. According to Fadlallah, "Lebanon was created by great powers in artificial borders, as the result of a political deal."[5] Lebanon's borders were tailored in an arbitrary fashion to create a bastion from which the West could continue to dominate the surrounding Muslim world. Lebanon "came into being to perform a specific mission for the West . . . to be a stage on which all the plans propounded for the region would be tested."[6]

Thus, says Fadlallah, there is nothing "eternal" about Lebanon, an entity that only exists and persists thanks to those "international political interests" that have a stake in its preservation. "But if the political situation in the region changes, not only is Lebanon unlikely to survive, neither will many other entities in the region."[7] When presidential elections became impossible in 1988, Subhi al-Tufayli declared, "I am astonished that there are those who say the sky will fall if elections for the presidency are not held, when we must eliminate the artificial entity known as Lebanon."[8] At Hezbollah's rallies contempt for the idea of Lebanon once took symbolic form in public burnings of the Lebanese flag. Fadlallah opposed such burnings as needlessly provocative and now the only flags burned are the American, Israeli and that of whichever European state is at odds with Iran at a given moment. Although Lebanon's flag is no longer burned, it is absent, supplanted by Iran's flag.

Yet Iran's flag is not flown as the national symbol of the Iranian state. The Iranian flag is regarded by its bearers in

---

[5]Interview with Fadlallah, *Der Spiegel*, April 1, 1985.

[6]Interview with Fadlallah, *al-Ittihad al-usbu'i* (Abu Dhabi), January 30, 1986.

[7]Interview with Fadlallah, *al-Nahar al-arabi wal-duwali*, March 10-16, 1986.

[8]Tufayli quoted by *al-Nahar*, July 15, 1988.

Hezbollah as the "flag of Islam."[9] Iran as a distinct state with its own state interests does not exist for Hezbollah. "They say to us, 'You are working in the interests of Iran' " says Hasan Nasrallah. "We say, 'Yes, we are working in the interests of an Iran that has no interests but Islam and the Muslims in the world.' "[10]

According to Ibrahim al-Amin, "The Iranian regime does not rule through Islam. Islam rules through the regime in Iran, and it will eventually rule the entire earth."[11] And Sayyid Ibrahim al-Amin emphasizes that, "the strategy in which the Muslims of Lebanon are fighting for with the revolution in Iran is not on behalf of the state of Iran; it is on behalf of Islam, which first burst forth in Iran."[12] He later reemphasized this by saying that, "We are not the 'pro-Iranian faction' in Lebanon. We are the faction of Islam, the faction of the Islamic revolution, the faction of the Imam-leader."[13]

The Islamic revolution first occurred in Iran, but it is not Iranian, as Sayyid Hasan Nasrallah declares: "the divine state of justice realized on part of this earth will not remain confined within its geographic borders, and is the dawn that will lead to the appearance of the *mahdi* [messiah], who will create the state of Islam on earth."[14] The fact that this "divine state of justice" began in Iran is of no particular significance, since it is destined to sweep across all the artificial frontiers that divide Islam. Hezbollah's clerics infrequently call the Islamic

---

[9]See the photographs of field units of the Islamic Resistance carrying Iranian flags, *al-Ahd*, December 26, 1986, and January 2 and 9, 1987. For a photograph of the use of the Iranian flag to drape the coffin of a "martyred" fighter, see *al-Ahd*, June 12, 1987.

[10]Speech by Hasan Nasrallah, *al-Ahd*, February 12, 1988.

[11]Speech by Ibrahim al-Amin, *al-Ahd*, February 12, 1988.

[12]Speech by Ibrahim al-Amin, *al-Ahd*, May 2, 1986.

[13]Speech by Ibrahim al-Amin, *al-Ahd*, February 12, 1988.

[14]Speech by Sayyid Hasan Nasrallah, *al-Ahd*, February 7, 1986.

Republic of Iran by its official name, since this connotes the existence of Iran as a discrete state. In Hezbollah's lexicon, the Islamic Republic of Iran is "Iran of Islam," *Iran al-Islam*, which suggests that Iran is one province of a greater Islam.

Just as Hezbollah refuses to countenance allegiance to Lebanon and Iran as states, so there is no place in Hezbollah's thought for Arab or Persian nationalisms, which divide Muslims along artificial lines. "We follow God and his religion of Islam, not Persia or the Arab nation," says Husayn al-Musawi. "If nationality and race obstruct Islamic links, then they are unacceptable."[15] An outspoken example of the rejection of Arabism may be found in a speech delivered by a local shaykh in south Lebanon during a visit by Iran's chargé d'affaires in Beirut:

> There is no Arab brotherhood or nationalist brotherhood here, because the Arabs have given us no aid despite the continuation of the crisis here for 10 years. Now they are cooperating with the satan whom they have brought to our country. The most unifying link is Islam. . . . Is it not Islam which has brought brother [Mahmud] Nurani [the Iranian chargé d'affaires] to us? Where are the Arabs? Why does the Persian come, but not the Arab? This demonstrates that the true tie between one man and another is that of thought and belief. We have no solidarity or common denominator with any being who does not believe in God and His prophet.[16]

## THE GREAT ISLAMIC STATE

Having renounced all allegiance to Lebanon, Iran and the Arab nation as the basis of sovereign self-expression, Hezbollah instead advocates the creation of what Sayyid Ibrahim al-

---

[15]Interview with Husayn al-Musawi, *al-Nahar al-arabi wal-duwali*, June 10-16, 1985.

[16]Speech by Shaykh Ibrahim Qusayr of Dayr Qanun al-Nahr, *al-Ahd*, February 28, 1986.

Amin calls a "great Islamic state" that will unite the entire region. Hezbollah seeks to incorporate Lebanon into a larger plan for establishing the rule of Islam wherever there are Muslims.[17] Hezbollah's manifesto describes Iran as the "nucleus of the world's central Islamic state."[18] The Islamic revolution in Iran gave birth to an idea, which has now become a plan for the entire Islamic nation. Just as Islamic Iran's message is Islamic in the broadest sense, so too is the mission of Hezbollah. "Our political work in Lebanon is not defined by the geography of Lebanon but by the geography of Islam, which is to say the geography of the world," says Ibrahim al-Amin.[19]

It is Hezbollah's position that an Islamic republic in Lebanon cannot be achieved until Lebanon is surrounded by a triumphant Islam. "We do not believe that it would be natural for an Islamic state to arise in Lebanon outside the plan," says Ibrahim al-Amin. "We wish Lebanon to be a part of the plan."[20] The establishment of an Islamic state in Lebanon "is not our demand," says Husayn al-Musawi. The aim is not Islam in one country, but the creation of an "all-encompassing Islamic state" that would include Lebanon.[21] Husayn al-Musawi has said that Hezbollah's victory in Lebanon depends upon "more struggles and confrontations with American imperialism and the Zionists. A prerequisite for establishing an Islamic government in Beirut is victory over the Zionist

---

[17]Interview with Ibrahim al-Amin, *al-Harakat al-Islamiyya fi Lubnan*, p.161.

[18]See "Nass al-risala al-maftuha," p.6.

[19]Interview with Ibrahim al-Amin, *al-Harakat al-Islamiyya fi Lubnan*, p.148.

[20]Interview with Ibrahim al-Amin, *al-Harakat al-Islamiyya fi Lubnan*, p.162.

[21]Interview with Husayn al-Musawi, *al-Harakat al-Islamiyya fi Lubnan*, pp.226-227.

regime, and this victory will be achieved through reliance on God."[22]

In a more oblique manner, Fadlallah has declared that "the Lebanese solution depends on a Middle East solution."[23] According to Ibrahim al-Amin, Lebanon's agony will end only "when the final Middle East map is drawn. We seek almighty God's help in drawing this map as soon as possible, with the blood of the martyrs and the strength of those who wage the *jihad* [holy war]."[24] This millenarian belief that a final map of the region is being drawn in blood sets the struggle of Hezbollah in an eschatological context for its adherents.

But it is not just millenarian belief that buttresses this strategic conception. A certain realism has led Hezbollah's spokesmen to conclude that an Islamic republic in Lebanon must be predicated upon Lebanon's inclusion in a larger Islamic state, which itself requires the success of Islamic revolution in adjacent lands. Lebanon is too small, its neighbors are too powerful and its Muslims are too divided to permit the establishment of an isolated Islamic republic in Lebanon. This is what Husayn al-Musawi means when he declares that "no person, Lebanese or Iranian, believes that what happened in Tehran can also occur in Beirut," and concludes that "it is not proper now to present a plan for the formation of an Islamic republic."[25]

There is a stark contrast between this strategy and the strategy of radical Islamic groups in Egypt, a much larger state and society than Lebanon. The leading theoreticians of Islamic revolution in Egypt speak first of transforming Egypt from within through some combination of persuasion and action. Only after Egypt is reconstituted as an Islamic state will

---

[22]Interview with Husayn al-Musawi, *Kayhan*, July 27, 1986.

[23]Interview with Fadlallah, *al-Ittihad* (Abu Dhabi), March 7, 1987.

[24]Interview with Ibrahim al-Amin, *Kayhan*, October 19, 1985.

[25]Interview with Husayn al-Musawi, *Kayhan*, July 27, 1986.

it have the wherewithal to embark on the mission of liberating
Jerusalem and uniting Islam. But Egypt is a large society
populated overwhelmingly by Muslims capable of sustaining
an Islamic republic, if a revolution brought one to power.

Lebanon is a small state populated by many sects and
surrounded by powerful states. The strategy of an Islamic order
in Lebanon must be predicated upon Lebanon's inclusion in a
larger Islamic entity, which itself requires the success of
Islamic revolution in adjacent lands. Hezbollah cannot
compromise over the pan-Islamic premises which guide it,
and is possibly more committed to these premises than Iran. At
some point, Islamic Iran may choose to set aside the
dissemination of its revolutionary message and settle for Islam
in one country. Islamic Iran can do so and persevere because it
also exists as an independent state with a broad demographic
and geographic base. But without the hope of an eventual
linkage with some larger Islamic political entity, the prospects
of an Islamic order in Lebanon are dim, and the sway of Islam
would remain confined to a few Beirut neighborhoods,
Hezbollah enclaves in the Bekaa Valley and south Lebanon.

Thus, the political course now being followed by Hezbollah
is not one that leads to the lesser aim of the Islamicization of
Lebanon. If this were indeed Hezbollah's immediate goal, a
first step might be the gradual inclusion of Hezbollah's agents
into the official institutions of the Lebanese state, with the
ultimate aim of bringing about an Islamic republic from
within. Yet Hezbollah has refused to employ this classic
revolutionary tactic. It professes no interest in the acquisition of
parliamentary seats and government positions, unlike its
Shi'ite rival Amal. It does not seek a solution to Lebanon's inter-
confessional conflict through a redistribution of offices among
Lebanon's religious communities.

There are people on the margins of Hezbollah who believe
that this attitude should be altered, and leaflets were circulated
in the southern suburbs of Beirut in late 1987, proposing that
Fadlallah be a candidate for the presidency of Lebanon. The
suggestion was dismissed by Fadlallah. In the words of one
Hezbollah spokesman, the movement "is not planning to take

over one post or another in the government, but is thinking about providing the groundwork to gain full political control."[26]

If Hezbollah's aims were limited to Lebanon, it might also have declared an Islamic republic in part of Lebanon as a prelude to total liberation. But this is another familiar tactic of revolutionary movements that Hezbollah has rejected. "Some groups in Lebanon have completed the structuring of their cantons," says Subhi al-Tufayli. "But let all hear this: We are not seeking to build any canton. We do not aspire to monopolize any part of Lebanon, neither in the western Bekaa Valley nor elsewhere. We realize that any political entity in the region must be under the Israeli umbrella in order to be allowed to exist. Hence, we do not think of any gains before the liberation of Palestine. There is nothing to be gained by anyone before that."[27] From time to time, rumors circulate that such a rump republic will soon be declared. Hezbollah's spokesmen immediately deny such rumors, which are probably intended to complicate Hezbollah's relations with Syria.

Certainly, if Hezbollah was determined to establish an Islamic republic in Lebanon, it would also have begun the process of delegitimizing Syria's presence there. The presence of a secular, Arab nationalist Syria is the most formidable obstacle to Lebanon's Islamicization. Although Hezbollah has established political and intellectual hegemony over the Shi'ites of the Bekaa Valley and Beirut, it must share control of these areas with Syrian forces.

Yet Hezbollah's militia has not only refrained from attacking Syria, its spokesmen have been careful not to openly criticize it despite Syria's growing encroachment on the strongholds of Hezbollah. More than fear is at work here. Hezbollah has deferred to Damascus because the larger

---

[26]Interview with Husayn al-Musawi, *Kayhan*, July 27, 1986. The movement will avoid taking posts "until it has gained control as a result of a mass revolution by the Muslim people."

[27]Interview with Subhi al-Tufayli, *al-Nahar al-arabi wal-duwali*, February 9-15, 1987.

strategy allots a prime role to cooperation with Syria in eradicating Israel. "Syria and Iran have a joint strategy based on the struggle against Israel and imperialism," Fadlallah recently reaffirmed.[28] "We would like to reiterate that our relationship with Damascus is a strategic one based on Syria's stands, which are hostile to Zionism and U.S. colonialism. . . . We believe any differences with Syria will not affect the agreement on principles governing our relationship, because we are all interested in decisively confronting the Zionist occupation through operations carried out by the Islamic Resistance."[29]

Fadlallah continued by saying, "We take a strategic view of relations with Syria. If problems occur from time to time, we do not believe they are serious enough to affect this strategic integration."[30] The tension with Syria has never been permitted to eclipse the primacy of the struggle against "global infidelity."

Finally, if Hezbollah was determined to win in Lebanon first, it might have devoted more resources to undermining the last vestiges of Christian hegemony. Yet while Hezbollah opposes Christian privilege, it has not invested its armed strength in fighting it. "We are fervent supporters of change," says Husayn al-Musawi, "but we have an order of priorities. The struggle against Israel takes precedence, because Israel is the largest and most dangerous enemy for us. Unfortunately, we do not have the means to struggle simultaneously against Israel and the Phalangist regime." Asked whether force of circumstance did not dictate this ordering of priorities, he replied, "Not at all. We could deploy our fighters along the separation line [between Christian and Muslim sectors] or on Jabal Sannin [overlooking the Christian enclave from the east].

---

[28]Interview with Fadlallah, *Le Quotidien de Paris*, March 9, 1987.

[29]Interview with Fadlallah, *al-Ittihad al-usbu'i*, July 2, 1987.

[30]Interview with Fadlallah, *al-Hawadith* (London), July 10, 1987.

We did not because we are convinced that Israel is the head of the viper, and it is Israel that we must strike."[31]

## DEFEAT AS DELAY

Until Iran's setbacks in the Gulf War and the 1988 cease-fire, Hezbollah's spokesmen described a victory over Iraq as the next step toward the realization of its vision. Husayn al-Musawi said that "as long as the banners of Islam do not wave over Baghdad and an Islamic government is not established in that land, the establishment of Islamic rule in Lebanon is not likely."[32] His statement reflected the widespread conviction in Hezbollah that the movement could not achieve its aims independently: Lebanon was an isolated island surrounded by forces hostile to Islam. Even if an Islamic republic was established there, it would not be viable as long as Hezbollah was not contiguous with the larger movement's consolidated base in Iran.

Hezbollah's spokesmen therefore emphasized regional victory instead of a victory in Lebanon. In thought and deed, Hezbollah accorded priority to the war between Iran and Iraq, which it described as a struggle between "truth and falsehood," on the assumption that an Iranian victory in the Gulf War would set the stage for Hezbollah's inevitable triumph.

The ultimate triumph of Islam in this contest was not in doubt. There were, of course, setbacks. According to Abbas al-Musawi, the overall "program of expansion" had been "delayed" by the course of the Gulf War.[33] But no one in Hezbollah openly doubted the ultimate triumph of Islam in this contest. "One day the Middle East will be in Muslim hands," affirmed Husayn al-Musawi.[34] Hezbollah's newspaper offered

---

[31]Interview with Husayn al-Musawi, *Nouveau Magazine*, July 23, 1988.

[32]Interview with Husayn al-Musawi, *Kayhan*, July 27, 1986.

[33]Interview with Abbas al-Musawi, *La Revue du Liban*, July 27-August 3, 1985.

[34]Interview with Husayn al-Musawi, *Le Figaro*, September 12, 1986.

exhaustive coverage of the innumerable Iranian offensives in the war, assuring readers that the victory of "the Islamic forces" was "only a matter of time."[35] For Hezbollah, the Iranian claim that the war was the first step toward the liberation of Jerusalem was not a rhetorical one, but reflected a divinely-ordained chronology. "Saddam will fall," declared Sayyid Ibrahim al-Amin during Iran's drive against the Iraqi city of Basra in early 1987. "We must ready ourselves to become soldiers in the army of Jerusalem."[36]

The obligation to obey Iran led Hezbollah to endorse what had been unthinkable: the July 1988 cease-fire between Iran and Iraq.[37] Khomeini's decision to accept U.N. resolution 598 had a demoralizing effect upon Hezbollah, which had viewed an Iranian victory as an essential condition for Hezbollah's progress. But an article in Hezbollah's monthly journal, explaining Khomeini's decision, put forward two arguments to justify it. One suggested that while the cease-fire signaled a military setback, martyrdom in the path of God had constituted a spiritual victory. The other proposed that the cease-fire was no more than an attempt to buy time and regroup, in accord with the precedents set by the Prophet Muhammad in the first wars of Islam.[38] God had not failed the Muslims, declared Husayn al-Musawi; all war was dynamic, and included successes and failures. Acceptance of the cease-fire did not spell the end of the war, and since Iraq was bound to block peace by acting as victor, Muslims had to redouble their efforts to prepare for the eventual victory of Islam.[39]

---

[35]See especially the coverage of the drive on Basra, *al-Ahd*, January 23, 1987.

[36]Speech by Ibrahim al-Amin, *al-Ahd*, January 23, 1987.

[37]Text of Hezbollah statement on Iran's acceptance of U.N. resolution 598, *al-Nahar*, July 22, 1988.

[38]See *al-Muntalaq* (Beirut), No.46 (September 1988), pp.58-70.

[39]Interview with Husayn al-Musawi, *Nouveau Magazine*, July 23, 1988.

But the Palestinian *intifadah* has been more effective at reinvigorating the movement. Since the cease-fire, the Gulf War has been replaced in Hezbollah's dominant discourse by events in Palestine, described by its spokesmen as the "Islamic *intifadah*." The rallies organized by Hezbollah, once devoted to the Gulf, are now devoted to solidarity with the *intifadah*, which is interpreted as a sign that the liberation of Jerusalem is not a distant dream.[40] Islam may have retreated in the Gulf, but it is advancing in Palestine, even under Israeli occupation. The outbreak of the uprising, with its Islamic overtones, has allowed the movement's thinkers to sustain their fundamental Islamic vision despite the Gulf War setback. Instead of reformulating their program in narrowly Lebanese terms, Hezbollah's spokesmen are engaged in a process of reformulating an Islamic vision that discounts the Gulf and fixes upon Palestine.

This was especially incongruous at a time when Hezbollah was investing the better part of its military energies in confrontations with Amal. In most respects, this was a typically Lebanese struggle between militia groups over the control of turf. Yet Hezbollah refused to define the conflict in narrowly Lebanese terms: it was conceived by Hezbollah's spokesmen not as part of the struggle for Lebanon, but as a chapter in the struggle to liberate Jerusalem. Hezbollah is committed to that liberation; Amal is not. Therefore, Hezbollah's struggle in Beirut's alleyways was really a battle for the redemption of Jerusalem. Hezbollah refuses to legitimate its struggle against Amal in Lebanese terms, as though Lebanon itself is not a worthy prize.

This Islamic perspective, even on the street battles of Beirut, invests profound purpose in every act of Hezbollah. By embracing the broadest perspective, Hezbollah fights not as a group of resentful men from an aggrieved sect in a small multi-confessional state. They fight as the Muslim vanguard of a worldwide struggle. Thus they transcend the narrow limits of confessional identity imposed upon them by the Lebanese state and "world arrogance." Removed from the context of a

---

[40]For accounts of such demonstrations, see *al-Ahd*, March 18, 1988.

wider Islamic struggle, Hezbollah would indeed be reduced to the sorry dimensions of a Lebanese militia—not soldiers in the "army of Jerusalem," but wayward bandits of Islam.

The allegiance professed to Khomeini's vision, the view of the Iranian revolution as the beginning of a worldwide Islamic revolution, the negation of nationalism and the anticipation that a great Islamic state will be created in this age are the doctrines that comprise the Islamic vision of Hezbollah. In the minds of those who elaborate this vision, there is nothing fantastic about these expectations, for this is a time of messianic redemption. No one believed that an Islamic state could be created against the will of the United States and the Soviet Union in Iran, yet it was done. No one believed that a few dedicated Muslims could drive out the Americans, French and Israelis from the heart of Lebanon, yet they did.

Fadlallah has called this the "rebellion against fear." The great powers inspire "alarm and fear" among the oppressed, who have no more than "children's toys" to mount their opposition. But by conquering their fear, through acceptance of the virtue of martyrdom, the oppressed can evoke alarm and fear among their oppressors.[41] America and the West, recalls one Hezbollah leader, "hurriedly ran away from three Muslims who loved martyrdom" and sacrificed themselves in suicidal attacks.[42] These successes are owed to the single-minded obedience of Hezbollah to Khomeini, his representatives and his successor, whose guidance is inspired if not infallible.

Sayyid Ibrahim al-Amin has assured Hezbollah that "those who blew up the Marine headquarters and the Israeli military governor in Tyre did not martyr themselves in accord with a decision by a political party or movement. They martyred themselves because the Imam Khomeini permitted them to do so. They saw nothing before them but God, and they defeated Israel and America for God. It was the imam of the nation

---

[41]Interview with Fadlallah, *al-Nahar al-arabi wal-duwali*, July 21-27, 1986.

[42]Interview with Sadiq al-Musawi, *al-Nahar al-arabi wal-duwali*, July 28-August 2, 1986.

[Khomeini] who showed them this path and instilled this spirit in them."[43]

At the root of Hezbollah's attitude toward the West is a confidence imparted by Hezbollah's victories in repeated confrontations with its adversaries in Lebanon. This is a movement whose members hold themselves to be under divine guidance and protection, and who believe that they will personally witness the advent of the millennium. The strategy of the movement is a "divine plan," and the leadership of Khomeini is a "divine opportunity."[44] Hezbollah's *ulama* are quite capable of making pragmatic calculations and do so all the time. But it is not pragmatism that inspires them. It is the anticipation of divine redemption that drives Hezbollah forward. Its portents are the humbling of Islam's timeless enemies.

---

[43]Speech by Ibrahim al-Amin, *al-Ahd*, January 23, 1987.

[44]Speech by Hasan Nasrallah, *al-Ahd*, February 12, 1988.

# IV   THE CONSPIRACY: ENEMIES OF ISLAM

The uproar over Salman Rushdie's *The Satanic Verses* sounded the depths of the resentment that fundamentalist Muslims bear against the West. This resentment is not only a reaction against the policies of individual Western governments, but a repudiation of Western power as a whole. In Hezbollah's vision, the present struggle is one more chapter in a saga of conflict between Islam and disbelief that transcends time. The confrontation manifests itself politically as a contest between imperialism and Islam. Fadlallah affirms that "our battle with imperialism is incessant and perpetual in order to weaken it, limit its interests and break its spine, exactly as imperialism endeavors to weaken poor peoples economically, politically, militarily, by all available means."[1]

Hezbollah affirms that events in Lebanon and the region are "not a contest over particularist gains or control or reforms, but a conflict between the defiant Islamic movement and Western and American interests."[2] But for Hezbollah, imperialism and its interests are but the latest manifestation of disbelief with which Islam has struggled since its inception. In Hezbollah's formulations, "global arrogance" (*al-istikbar al-*

---

[1]Interview with Fadlallah, *Middle East Insight*, March-April 1988.

[2]Hezbollah statement, *al-Ahd*, April 22, 1988.

*alami*)—which might be roughly understood as imperialism—
is synonymous with "global infidelity" (*al-kufr al-alami*).

From a theoretical point of view, Hezbollah regards the
West as unified, and assumes that Western opposition to its
vision is conditioned by a sense of ancient religious rivalry. To
Hezbollah, political differences that divide the West are
insignificant compared to the religious and cultural chasm
that separates Islam from the West. Among the strategists of
the movement, there is a recognition that the West, like Islam,
has its internal differences, and that these differences can be
used to the advantage of Islam. Hezbollah has sought out the
points of weakness, of half-resolve, of division in the West, and
has sought to exploit them for the benefit of the cause.

But the ideological underpinning of this policy accords
with an adage attributed to the prophet: "infidelity is one
nation." The banner headline of Hezbollah's newspaper
evoked those words at the height of the Gulf crisis in the
summer of 1987: "An Attack of Infidelity (*kufr*) in its Entirety
against Faith (*iman*) in its Entirety."[3] Hasan Nasrallah says
that, "The struggle in the world today is between the Islamic
plan and the infidel plan led by America and Russia."[4] In
graphic form a wall poster in Beirut signed by Hezbollah
shows "global infidelity" as a fanged monster in semi-human
form: one eye is filled with the American stars and stripes,
another with the Soviet hammer and sickle, and its flesh is
made of the Union Jack and Tricolor. The hand of Islam
reaches up to throttle the creature.[5] The enemies of Islam at
times may disagree among themselves, but the West remains

---

[3]*Al-Ahd*, July 24, 1987.

[4]Speech by Nasrallah, *al-Ahd*, March 18, 1988.

[5]Reproduced in Wright, *Sacred Rage*, facing p.68. Wall posters are also
texts, presenting graphic representations of the themes that dominate
Hezbollah's discourse. Hezbollah's posters draw heavily upon Iranian
models. See William J. Hanaway Jr., "The Symbolism of Persian
Revolutionary Posters," in Barry M. Rosen, ed., *Iran since the Revolution*
(Boulder, Col.: Social Science Monographs, 1985), pp.31-50, 150-172.
Compare with the report on a Hezbollah-sponsored Islamic art and
portraiture exhibit in *al-Ahd*, February 2, 1986.

collectively hostile to Islam, and Islam must unite to confront a united adversary.

Hezbollah's rage against the West is exemplified by the treatment that its covert affiliates have accorded to hostages and hijacked plane passengers. The brutality and sustained intimidation displayed by Shi'ite captors and hijackers reveal much about the systematic indoctrination employed by the movement. These members of Hezbollah's covert branch have conducted themselves not simply as people aggrieved by the policies of certain governments, but as believers who readily displace their rage upon anything or anyone who remotely represents "global infidelity." The assumptions upon which this rage rests are not self-taught. Their origins lay in the systematic indoctrination offered by Hezbollah's *ulama* in open preaching—a preaching which, despite its nuances, has constituted an incitement as powerful as the ruling of Khomeini against Rushdie.

Hezbollah's vision of the West is formed by a wide range of influences. The least of these has been direct cross-cultural contact. Many leading figures in Hezbollah have visited the West, some know one of its languages. On the whole, they are more worldy than the Iranian emissaries in their midst. But like the popular Western understanding of Islam, Hezbollah's understanding of the West draws upon a reservoir of prejudices formed by past conflict and reinforced by present-day strife. Indoctrination builds upon a firm foundation of beliefs about the secret power of the West, its desire to subjugate Islam and the Muslims, and its use of Jews, Christian minorities and apostates from Islam to accomplish its aims. Much of Hezbollah's discourse on the West evokes medieval Islamic discourse, although it also reflects the influence of the modern secular self-indictment of the West. There is also some variation in how spokesmen understand the West, since they are not uniformly knowledgeable about the outside world.

Much of this indoctrination is specific to different Western countries. A great deal of political, military and diplomatic interaction has occurred between Hezbollah and the Western governments, including complex indirect negotiations over the fate of Western hostages. The purpose here is not to recount this history, but to capture the image of each of Hezbollah's Western adversaries as projected by Hezbollah's spokesmen. These images serve to sanction acts against Western governments and their nationals by overtly defining the legitimate targets of Hezbollah's covert struggle. While these definitions are not as specific as Khomeini's ruling against Salman Rushdie, they perform the same broad purpose of identifying the enemies of Islam for all those true Muslims who find themselves in a position to strike a blow for the cause.

## AMERICA: "FIRST ROOT OF VICE"

Islam is one pole of Hezbollah's world, the United States is the other. It is the great adversary that Hezbollah must defeat if its vision is to be realized. The task of uniting Islam has fallen to Iran, in partnership with Hezbollah. The task of uniting the West has been assumed by the United States. In that sense, the decisive conflict in the contemporary world is not between the great powers, but between Islam and the West, and especially between Islam and the United States. "The scene must either be controlled by the United States or dominated by Islam," says Ibrahim al-Amin.[6]

Few Americans would recognize themselves or their nation as they are portrayed by Hezbollah. The United States is a "world-devouring" imperialist power that directs what Ibrahim al-Amin calls a "network of influence" throughout the Middle East. The United States employs this network in a devious manner, to divide the Muslim world and thoroughly dominate it. As Ibrahim al-Amin has explained, "we do not want this separation to be achieved, because we are part of the nation of Islam. America is itself aware of the fact that our fight in Lebanon against it is part of the fight of the nations of the region, and we will fight America everywhere in the region and the world. For America is not only the enemy of Lebanon

---

[6]Interview with Ibrahim al-Amin, *Jomhuri-ye Islami* (Tehran), April 20, 1986.

and the Palestinians. It is the foremost enemy of all the Muslims of the world."[7]

The view of the United States articulated by Hezbollah is of an arrogant power possessing a clear plan of action for oppressing and subordinating the region's peoples. The policy of the United States toward the Middle East is not only coherent, but reaches sinister levels of conspiratorial deceit. The spokesmen of Hezbollah attribute all of the region's misfortunes to a successful manipulation of events by the United States, working either through its own agencies or regional surrogates. "We are proceeding toward a battle with vice at its very roots," reads Hezbollah's manifesto. "And the first root of vice is America." The manifesto goes on to remind readers that "the Imam Khomeini, our leader, has repeatedly stressed that America is the cause of all our catastrophes and the source of all malice."[8]

Hezbollah's manifesto vows to defeat this conspiracy: "We will turn Lebanon into a graveyard for American schemes."[9] Subhi al-Tufayli declares that, "We want to tell the United States that we will be very happy when the war between us and them starts face to face. We are proud to be the point of the Muslim spear in the chest of U.S. authority. Thus, we welcome any U.S. return [to Lebanon] because this will give us the opportunity to fight it more effectively."[10] And Hezbollah spokesman Sadiq al-Musawi vows that, "If the Americans and the West one day should decide on a quick death, let them please come, for those who love martyrdom will be waiting for them. But we would like to impress on them that they should

---

[7]Interview with Ibrahim al-Amin, *Kayhan*, February 9, 1986.

[8]See "Nass al-risala al-maftuha," p.9.

[9]See "Nass al-risala al-maftuha," p.17.

[10]Interview with Subhi al-Tufayli, *al-Nahar al-arabi wal-duwali*, February 9-15, 1987.

bring their own coffins with them so that the scattered bodies will not be lying about for too long."[11]

This powerful anti-American sentiment reflects Hezbollah's resentment of a U.S. Middle East policy opposed to Iran and supportive of Israel and the moderate Arab states. In Hezbollah's view, the United States is actively working to defeat the spread of Islam. But opposition to U.S. policies is not the whole of Hezbollah's anti-Americanism. Many in Hezbollah also regard the United States as the foremost representative of a rival civilization, engaged in a perpetual confrontation with the civilization of Islam. Opposition to specific U.S. policies gives Hezbollah a precise focus for its anti-Americanism. But Hezbollah's view of the United States as champion of the West allows the movement to regard its struggle not simply as a reaction to the policies of one state, but as a chapter in the continuing *jihad* of Islam against "global infidelity." This satisfies the same need as Khomeini's identification of the United States as the "Great Satan"—an identification that goes beyond resentment of U.S. policy and serves to place the locus of all evil outside the pure core of Islam.[12]

That is not to say that there is no nuance in the views of some in Hezbollah regarding the conduct of the struggle against the United States. Fadlallah has argued that Hezbollah should limit its struggle to a campaign against U.S. policy and his approach has been to downplay the broader aspects of the conflict. "I do not take a negative view of relations with the big powers," says Fadlallah. "We, as a community that is part of this world, should have positive relations with all the world's countries. We must make sure that our relations with the United States should not be those between a slave and his

---

[11]Interview with Sadiq al-Musawi, *al-Nahar al-arabi wal-duwali*, July 28-August 2, 1986.

[12]William O. Beeman, "Images of the Great Satan: Representations of the United States in the Iranian Revolution," in Nikki Keddie, ed., *Religion and Politics in Iran* (New Haven: Yale University Press, 1983), pp.191-217.

master, or between a master and a satellite. . . . We appreciate that the United States and other countries have their interests in the world. We have no wish to jeopardize their interests, but it is our right not to allow their interests to destroy our interests."[13]

For Fadlallah, an emphasis on the civilizational aspect of the struggle can only align American opinion behind the hateful policies of the U.S. government, and he has consistently sought to reassure Americans that their own values, beliefs and personal security arc not under threat. "We are not against the American and European peoples, and we wish to be friendly with all nations, because this is one of the commandments of Almighty God," he said. "We will confront American and European policies, however, because these policies are based on crushing oppressed nations."[14] On another occasion he declared that, "We are not against the American people. On the contrary, we have many friends in the United States, and consider its inhabitants a naturally good, tolerant people. Yet we oppose the U.S. administration's policy, which has been the root cause of many of our problems and those of the American people."[15]

The distinction that Fadlallah draws between the American people and its government has led him to withhold sanction of the kidnapping of individual Americans. Fadlallah has not mounted a public campaign against hostage-taking, nor has he compromised the security of the hostage-holders by revealing what he knows about them. His diplomacy has been discreet and discriminating. It has rested not on criticism, but on the withholding of sanction: "We do not justify the

---

[13]Interview with Fadlallah, *al-Nahar al-arabi wal-duwali,* July 1-7, 1985.

[14]Holiday prayer sermon by Fadlallah, quoted by Radio Tehran, June 21, 1985, in Foreign Broadcast Information Service: Daily Report, Middle East (henceforth, FBIS/ME), June 21, 1985.

[15]Fadlallah, "Islam and Violence in Political Reality," *Middle East Insight,* Vol.4, Nos.4-5 (1986), p.13.

kidnapping of American citizens who might have nothing to do with their government or might be opposed to it."[16]

But on no issue has Fadlallah's subtlety had less of an impact on Hezbollah than the question of kidnapping and the detention of innocents. Fadlallah's purpose, he once claimed, was to "create a psychological situation that would bring pressure to bear on the kidnappers themselves."[17] This he has failed to do. The counter-concept of "open war" (*ma'raka maftuha*) against the United States has been best articulated by Ibrahim al-Amin. Angered at the criticism of kidnapping by certain unnamed Shi'ites, Ibrahim al-Amin asked why they criticize kidnapping more often than they denounce the "crimes" of America and Israel. The battle waged by Hezbollah is an "open" one, he declared, and the oppressed have a right to confront the United States "with the relevant methods they choose."[18]

As Ibrahim al-Amin reminded his audience, Khomeini did not condemn kidnapping in Lebanon, and he acquiesced in the 1979 takeover of the U.S. Embassy in Tehran. "The imam neither protested this action nor said it was wrong."[19] For Ibrahim al-Amin, this is inferential evidence that kidnapping is a permissible means of political struggle. As Hezbollah's newspaper again recently reminded readers, "the Muslims of Iran held Americans hostage for 444 days, and

---

[16]Interview with Fadlallah, *al-Nahar al-arabi wal-duwali*, July 1-7, 1985. For a fuller analysis of Fadlallah's position on hostage-taking, see Kramer, *The Moral Logic of Hizballah*. This position, combined with the certainty that Fadlallah has detailed knowledge of hostage-holding, has made him a regular stop in the itineraries of the families of hostages and hostage negotiators. They are rewarded with meandering monologues of dissimulation. For an embittered account of one such audience, by the wife of a French hostage who later died in captivity, see Marie Seurat, *Les Corbeaux d'Alep* (Paris: Gallimard, 1988), pp. 22-24.

[17]Interview with Fadlallah, *al-Hawadith*, March 27, 1987.

[18]Ibrahim al-Amin speech quoted by United Press International, June 30, 1987.

[19]Ibrahim al-Amin speech quoted by UPI, June 30, 1987.

they did not free them until America bowed completely to the Islamic Republic's demands."[20] Although Ibrahim al-Amin might have had doubts about the morality of his own position, given the personal innocence of certain American hostages, the interests of Islam took precedence: "Regardless of whether the kidnappers are wrong or right, we will never support or defend the U.S. or its enemy's positions on the hostage issue. . . . We will not adopt stands against the oppressed, even if they commit mistakes."[21] But many in Hezbollah did not entertain the slightest doubts. Shaykh Zuhayr Kanj, a Hezbollah cleric closely identified with hostage-holding, returned from Khomeini's funeral in Iran and declared that, "The detention of the hostages is a humiliation for the Bush administration and a source of pride for Muslims." He called for their continued detention "even if the United States unblocks the Iranian assets."[22]

Therefore, Hezbollah's war against the United States knows no theoretical moral limits in the minds of many who wage it. In February 1987, when West Germany arrested a Lebanese Shi'ite suspected of involvement in the hijacking of a TWA flight to Beirut in June 1985, Husayn al-Musawi came to his defense by insisting that even if the suspect was guilty, "so what? We are at open war with the Americans, their planes, their cars, their people, and the Germans should keep out of it."[23] According to an editorial in Hezbollah's newspaper, "the United States is the Great Satan, and there must be no leniency in the war against it."[24] The only restraints are practical ones

---

[20]Editorial in *al-Ahd*, March 4, 1988.

[21]Ibrahim al-Amin, quoted by the Voice of the Oppressed (clandestine), June 28, 1989.

[22]Shaykh Zuhayr Kanj, quoted by the Agence France-Presse (Sidon), June 13, 1989, in FBIS/ME, June 14, 1989.

[23]Husayn al-Musawi quoted by Deutsche Presse Aggentur (Beirut), February 4, 1987, in FBIS/ME, February 5, 1987.

[24]Editorial in *al-Ahd*, March 4, 1988.

stemming from Hezbollah's limited resources and considerations of timing.

The question of timing is now a paramount one, as Iran and Hezbollah consider their strategic options. Fadlallah has always favored an Iranian opening to the United States, and the use of guile rather than force to diminish the stature of the United States in the Middle East. "It is possible to establish balanced relations with the Washington administration," he has declared, provided that Iran seeks such a dialogue "from a declared position of strength." Islamic Iran did as much when it worked to secure arms from the United States.[25] Others in Hezbollah disagree, convinced that the "oppressed" cannot negotiate with the United States from a position of strength, and that the cause is better served by uninterrupted confrontation. "The Islamic revolution asserts rejection of America and the refusal to deal with it," Husayn al-Musawi has affirmed.[26] In the minds of others, rejection is not sufficient. During a speech to a Beirut Hezbollah procession after Khomeini's death, Sayyid Hasan Nasrallah urged Hezbollah to "satisfy our imam's desire by announcing the beginning of the real war against the United States."[27]

Dialogue, hostage-holding and war are but alternative approaches for the achievement of one goal: the elimination of American influence in the Muslim world. The episodes of pragmatic restraint in the policy of Hezbollah are due to the asymmetry of power between Islam and the United States which favors the latter. But the asymmetry cannot last. "We might not have the actual power the U.S. has," admits Fadlallah, "but we had the power previously and we have now the foundations to develop that power in the future. We might wait 20, 30 or 40 years before we will be able to attain that

---

[25]Interview with Fadlallah, *La Vanguardia*, November 9, 1986; quoted in FBIS/ME, November 17, 1986.

[26]Interview with Husayn al-Musawi, *al-Nahar al-arabi wal-duwali*, October 28-November 3, 1985.

[27]Report on Hezbollah's "farewell procession" for Khomeini in Beirut, Voice of the Oppressed (clandestine), June 6, 1989.

power."[28] Until that time, Hezbollah cannot acquiesce in the present distribution of world power, a distribution that gives the United States a decisive say in the fate of hundreds of millions of Muslims. Since Fadlallah tends to speak of longer time frames than other Hezbollah spokesmen, it is likely that many in Hezbollah expect revolutionary Islam to emerge as a world power in less time.

Just as power shifted in this century from Western Europe to the United States and the Soviet Union, it is bound to shift in the next century to the "oppressed of the earth" and particularly to the Muslims. The Islamic vision of Hezbollah is predicated upon the decline of American power. The rise of revolutionary Islam will come principally at the expense of the United States.

## ISRAEL: "WATCHDOG OF AMERICAN IMPERIALISM"

The United States has not yet committed its forces to a decisive confrontation with Hezbollah because it has a proxy in the form of Israel. In the mind of Hezbollah, Israel exists to execute American policy. "As for Israel," says Hezbollah's manifesto, "we consider it the American spearhead in our Islamic world."[29] According to Ibrahim al-Amin, Israel "acts as an American tool which exists for the purpose of striking out at Muslims in the region."[30] According to Abbas al-Musawi, "We believe that the Middle East has always been under the eye of two watchdogs of American imperialism: the shah of Iran and Israel. Thank God we were able to get rid of the shah."[31] The wars waged by Israel are actually America's wars. One cannot "interpret the barefaced American aggression against Iran without reference to the American

[28]Interview with Fadlallah, *Middle East Insight*, March-April 1988.

[29]See "Nass al-risala al-maftuha," p.28.

[30]Interview with Ibrahim al-Amin, *Kayhan*, February 9, 1987.

[31]Interview with Abbas al-Musawi, *La Revue du Liban*, July 27–August 3, 1985.

assault against the Islamic resistance in south Lebanon."[32] Few in Hezbollah subscribe to the notion, so prevalent in many Arab views of the American-Israeli relationship, that it is Israel that runs U.S. policy toward the Middle East.

Instead, it is American rather than Israeli objectives that Israel pursues. When Israeli forces invaded Lebanon, it was at America's behest: "The Israeli invasion of Lebanon was the product of an American-Israeli plan. Perhaps Israel did not want to advance to Beirut, but the American plan forced it to do so, in order to encircle the PLO and oust it from the city."[33] When Israel bombed PLO headquarters in Tunis, the operation was supervised by the United States: "We are certain that this operation was jointly planned and implemented by the United States and Israel under the supervision of the CIA," says Islamic Jihad. "The Israelis were supplied with fuel from the U.S. warships in the Mediterranean Sea and given information about Tunis."[34]

When Israel finally did withdraw from most of Lebanon, the decision was made in Washington: "As long as the Americans stand to gain from the Israelis remaining in south Lebanon, they will remain," says Fadlallah. "And when the Americans stand to gain from them withdrawing, they will withdraw."[35] The Israeli withdrawal to a "security zone" in south Lebanon was a product of an American decision: "If it were only up to Israel, its occupation would continue," says Fadlallah. "However, the Americans need something they can offer to the so-called moderate Arab regimes who are working on a peaceful solution to the Palestinian conflict."[36] Israel, according to Fadlallah, does not have complete freedom

---

[32]Hezbollah statement, *al-Ahd*, April 22, 1988.

[33]Fadlallah, "Islam and Violence in Political Reality," p.13.

[34]Islamic Jihad announcement of William Buckley's "execution," *al-Nahar*, October 4, 1985.

[35]Interview with Fadlallah, *Le Quotidien de Paris*, September 23, 1986.

[36]Interview with Fadlallah, *Der Spiegel*, April 1, 1985.

to act in Lebanon because that would "embarrass many of the 'American Arabs' who are working to pave the way for American schemes."[37] Most recently, Hezbollah accused the United States of masterminding Israel's abduction of Shaykh Abd al-Karim Ubayd.

This leads Hezbollah to argue that by pressuring the United States, Israel can be made to yield. "When the people in Lebanon, particularly those who are politically active, see the United States giving great military and political support to Israel through the U.S.-Israeli strategic alliance, it is natural that when they think of applying pressure on Israel, they will also think of applying pressure on the United States so that it will then bring pressure to bear on Israel."[38] Hezbollah does not imagine itself capable of driving a wedge between the United States and Israel: the United States would not sever its own arm. Hezbollah's strategy is predicated on the assumption that the United States and Israel react as one. By this understanding of the relationship between the United States and Israel, Hezbollah ultimately reaffirms its belief in the unity of Islam's enemies, under the supreme guidance of the United States. As Ibrahim al-Amin explains, "all the wars, destruction, carnage and massacres which have occurred in the course of history or in the recent decade are as a result of the political, economic and military support of the United States for Israel."[39]

Fadlallah also regards Israel as the servant of American interests. "We are aware of the Israeli-U.S. connection," says Fadlallah. "It is aimed at turning the entire region here into a U.S.-Israeli zone of influence, as required by the strategic, political and economic interests of the United States."[40] The relationship, according to Fadlallah, functions in this manner: "America acts diplomatically and tells Israel to move

---

[37]Interview with Fadlallah, *al-Ittihad al-usbu'i*, January 30, 1986.

[38]Interview with Fadlallah, *al-Nahar al-arabi wal-duwali*, July 1-7, 1985.

[39]Interview with Ibrahim al-Amin, *Kayhan*, October 19, 1985.

[40]Interview with Fadlallah, *Der Spiegel*, April 1, 1985.

militarily. . . . America suggests peace and leaves Israel to suggest war, so that if anyone rebels against the American peace, he is threatened with an Israeli war."[41]

On the other hand, Fadlallah also believes that the Jews would like to exercise their own power: "The Jews want to be a world superpower. . . . No one should imagine that the Jews act on behalf of any super or minor power. It is their personality to make for themselves a future world presence."[42] But this contradictory analysis, which apparently owes its genesis to Fadlallah's exposure to ideological anti-Semitism, is not in accord with the dominant discourse of Hezbollah, which portrays Israel as an extension of American will.[43]

Nevertheless, even if Israel was not an instrument of the United States, Hezbollah would oppose its existence as a matter of Islamic principle. According to Fadlallah, Israel cannot be viewed "as a state with the right to security and peace just like any other state in the region. We cannot see Israel as a legal presence, considering that it is a conglomeration of people who came from all parts of the world to live in Palestine on the ruins of another people."[44] No process can confer legitimacy on Israel. The United Nations cannot do so; indeed, "even if the Jews should suddenly become Muslims, we would ask them to leave Palestine, which was usurped by them."[45] As Husayn al-Musawi explains, "we and our Iranian brothers cannot accept Israel's existence. It is the Palestinians' land. The Israelis must leave and find somewhere else. We must struggle against Israel's existence. Palestine is not the Jews' home."[46]

---

[41]Fadlallah Friday sermon, *al-Ahd*, December 6, 1985.

[42]Fadlallah interview, *Middle East Insight*, March-April 1988.

[43]Fadlallah believes in the veracity of the *Protocols of the Elders of Zion*; Carré, "Quelques mots-clefs," p.491.

[44]Interview with Fadlallah, *Monday Morning*, September 14, 1986.

[45]Interview with Fadlallah, *Der Spiegel*, April 1, 1985.

[46]Interview with Husayn al-Musawi, *Le Figaro*, September 12, 1986.

It has been argued that when Hezbollah speaks of liberating Jerusalem, its purpose is primarily to mobilize support for the seizure of power in Lebanon and the establishment of an Islamic state in Lebanon. In this view, the "rhetorical insistence on liberation comes second in the order of priorities of the Islamic movement," and the liberation of south Lebanon "is considered second to an essential goal, the establishment of an Islamic state. In that, the Islamic groups are not different from any other of the groups of the Lebanese civil wars scene."[47] But Hezbollah's "insistence" is far from rhetorical: Israel is not only an injustice, but a mortal danger. According to Fadlallah, "Israel's ambitions to extend from the Euphrates to the Nile are known. . . . We can never have any security, whether military, economic or political, as long as Israel is harboring its expansionist designs."[48]

Subhi al-Tufayli affirms that "we cannot have independent and free countries in our Arab world as long as Israel exists. Any of us who want to lead a dignified life must first purge the land of Palestine of Jews. It is on this basis that we reject any truce or peace with Israel."[49] Only a radical cure will do. As al-Tufayli has said, "Palestine will be liberated by arms and not by negotiation."[50] Husayn al-Musawi has said the same: "Israel will disappear through battle sooner or later." It is a

---

[47]See Chibli Mallat, *Shi'i Thought from the South of Lebanon* (Oxford: Centre for Lebanese Studies, 1988), pp. 36-37. Mallat does not consider the issue of the great Islamic state, since he assumes that Hezbollah's aim "in theory" is the establishment of an Islamic republic. Hezbollah's manifesto, however, makes no reference to an Islamic republic in Lebanon.

[48]Interview with Fadlallah, *al-Nahar al-arabi wal-duwali*, July 1-7, 1985.

[49]Interview with Subhi al-Tufayli, *al-Nahar al-arabi wal-duwali*, February 9-15, 1987.

[50]Subhi al-Tufayli quoted by Agence France-Presse, May 23, 1987, in FBIS/ME, May 26, 1987.

"cancer that must be cut out of this nation's body"[51] and a "germ that must not be given a truce. Otherwise, we will have given it the chance to destroy us."[52] Abbas al-Musawi also terms Israel "the cancer of the Middle East. . . . In the future, we will wipe out every trace of Israel in Palestine," he said.[53] "Our actions will continue until we enter the very heart of Palestine, for our goal is not the liquidation of [South Lebanese Army Commander] Antoine Lahad in the border zone. Our slogan is the liquidation of Israel."[54]

According to Hasan Nasrallah, "We must drive Israel from our country, not in order to stop the battle when we reach the border, but to continue the battle to Jerusalem."[55] Fadlallah says that disengagement agreements and security arrangements cannot solve the problem, for "the question is not one of the borders between us and Israel."[56] Ibrahim al-Amin concurs, saying that, "There is no way of secure coexistence with the Zionist entity. There will be no solution to the Palestine question and no peace in the region until Israel ceases to exist."[57] He recently reiterated this by saying that, "The Zionist entity is nothing but a cancerous growth which is striving to infiltrate the area gradually. Therefore, the only solution that will lead to security and just and lasting peace in the region

---

[51]Interview with Husayn al-Musawi, *al-Nahar al-arabi wal-duwali*, June 10-16, 1985.

[52]Interview with Husayn al-Musawi, *al-Ittihad*, December 12, 1986.

[53]Interview with Abbas al-Musawi, *La Revue du Liban*, July 27-August 3, 1985.

[54]Speech by Abbas al-Musawi, *as-Safir* (Beirut), September 23, 1986.

[55]Speech by Hasan Nasrallah, *al-Ahd*, February 12, 1988.

[56]Speech by Fadlallah, *al-Ahd*, March 25, 1988.

[57]Statement by Ibrahim al-Amin at news conference, *al-Ahd*, January 8, 1988.

lies in the total removal of this cancerous growth."[58] This is the reason Husayn al-Musawi has declared that "a prerequisite for establishing Islamic government in Beirut is victory over the Zionist regime, and this victory will be achieved through reliance on God."[59]

This does not mean that Hezbollah expects to liberate Palestine in the same way that it liberated parts of Lebanon. As Fadlallah has explained, the struggle of Hezbollah against Israel in Lebanon was meant to "make confrontation with Israel possible in the future on the grounds that Israel is not an irresistible power even if it is supported by the United States." But as Fadlallah has recognized, "there is a difference between the liberation of Palestine and the liberation of south Lebanon as far as the method of operation is concerned." The liberation of Palestine requires the emergence of an Islamic resistance there, and an "Arab-Islamic plan for confrontation." Without such a plan, operations against Israel from Lebanon would become "mere acts of self-martyrdom. That is why we think differently about the post-Israeli withdrawal phase, differently from the way of the resistance in south Lebanon."[60]

Although the Islamic Resistance achieved most of its aims in Lebanon within a few years, Fadlallah believes that Israel's elimination cannot be achieved in "one, two or 10 years," but that "we must persecute Israel for 100 years if necessary."[61] One day, says Fadlallah, Jerusalem will be returned, but "in this connection we think of great periods of time."[62]

But this does not mean that Hezbollah can postpone the struggle against Israel to some distant day. For Hezbollah, the *jihad* against Israel cannot be suspended but must be conducted

---

[58]Ibrahim al-Amin, quoted by the Voice of the Oppressed (clandestine), June 28, 1989.

[59]Interview with Husayn al-Musawi, *Kayhan*, July 27, 1986.

[60]Interview with Fadlallah, *al-Hawadith*, May 24, 1985.

[61]Interview with Fadlallah, *Monday Morning*, September 14, 1986.

[62]Interview with Fadlallah, *Der Spiegel*, April 1, 1985.

as a continuing war of attrition until it evolves into a war of liberation. Ibrahim al-Amin has outlined the four stages of a strategic "plan" that includes confrontation with Israel ("the basic foundation"), the toppling of the Lebanese regime, the liberation of Lebanon from political and military intervention by the great powers and the establishment of Islam as the basis of rule, "until the Muslims of Lebanon join with the Muslims throughout the world in this age, to implement the single Islamic plan, and so become the centralized, single nation (*umma*) willed by God, who decreed that 'your nation will be one.' "[63] Confrontation, unlike the subsequent three stages, is a process. But nothing else can be achieved unless it rests upon "the basic foundation" of a continuous struggle against Israel.

Recent events convinced many members of Hezbollah that the liberation of Jerusalem might not be as remote as Fadlallah imagines: Israel is beginning to unravel in the face of the "Islamic *intifadah*." The Palestinian uprising is a confirmation of Israel's fundamental weaknesses first revealed in the successful Islamic struggle to expel Israel from most of south Lebanon. Fadlallah recognizes that the *intifadah* is not being conducted only by Palestinians "who adhere to the line of Islam," but it is nonetheless "inspired by the spirit of Islam." It was the introduction of an Islamic dimension to the Palestinian struggle that uprooted fear from Palestinian hearts. Fadlallah has said that, "The uprising is a preparatory step toward revolution in the future."[64]

Hezbollah has organized many rallies in solidarity with the *intifadah*, emphasizing to its followers that the liberation of Jerusalem is not a distant dream.[65] Hezbollah's advice to those who are conducting the *intifadah* "in the depths of the Zionist entity" is to define their aims and choose their leadership in

---

[63]Speech by Ibrahim al-Amin, *al-Ahd*, December 6, 1986.

[64]Interview with Fadlallah, *al-Haqiqa* (Beirut), December 24, 1987.

[65]See *al-Ahd*, March 18, 1988.

accord with the slogan: "Israel must cease to exist."[66] Hezbollah has always had ties to what one Hezbollah leader called "religious and Muslim Palestinians who are ready to fight Israel. In fact we and they have carried out joint operations."[67] Since the *intifadah* began, Hezbollah has established numerous ties to the Palestinian Islamic Jihad movement. These groups have become closer since the beginning of the uprising and the expulsion of several Palestinian Islamic activists to Lebanon.

At the same time, Hezbollah has opposed all attempts to translate the *intifadah* into a political process, calling instead for its escalation into a full-blown *jihad*. Hezbollah condemned the declaration of Palestinian independence made by the Palestine National Council that met in Algiers in November 1988. Acceptance of U.N. resolution 181 from 1948 meant forfeiture of most of the Palestinian soil to the Zionist enemy, whereas it was incumbent upon Palestinians to "liberate all the holy Islamic soil and eliminate Israel from existence." Hezbollah "reiterates its willingness to cooperate with all revolutionary forces that reject the principle of negotiation with the Zionist enemy and endorse the method of armed *jihad*."[68]

In December 1988, Hezbollah convened in Beirut what it called the "First World Conference in Support of the Islamic *Intifadah* in Occupied Palestine." The gathering, which reiterated the demand for Israel's liquidation, was also attended by the Palestinian rejectionists Ahmad Jibril and Abu Musa.[69] Their presence at the conference, and their subsequent publicized contacts with Hezbollah and Iran, indicated that a broad common ground of cooperation had been established between Hezbollah and Palestinian rejectionism. In its early years, Hezbollah enjoyed very good relations with Yasser

---

[66]Press conference statement by Ibrahim al-Amin, *al-Ahd*, January 8, 1988; speech by Ibrahim al-Amin, *al-Ahd*, March 4, 1988.

[67]Interview with Husayn al-Musawi, *al-Majallah*, April 8-14, 1987.

[68]Text of statement, *al-Nahar*, November 19, 1988.

[69]Account of conference, *al-Alam* (London), January 7, 1989.

Arafat's Fatah, partly on the basis of a shared antipathy to Amal. Few of those ties remain.[70]

Hezbollah believes that Israel will cease to exist when Islam emerges as a world power. For Hezbollah, the destruction of Israel and the decline of American power are inextricably linked and will occur in tandem. When the map of the Middle East is redrawn "in blood," Palestine will be part and parcel of what Hezbollah, following Khomeini, calls the "great Islamic state," constructed on the ruins of America's Israel.

## WEST EUROPE: "SUBSERVIENT TO THE UNITED STATES"

Before World War II, Muslims associated the West not with the United States but Europe. Islam's great confrontation with the West had been a confrontation with Europe, culminating in the establishment of European imperial rule over most of the Muslim world. As decolonization proceeded, the United States and the Soviet Union began to project their growing power in the Muslim world, and Europe generally ceased to serve as a focus of hostility.

But while Hezbollah's spokesmen regard Israel as an American instrument to dominate Islam, they view most of Western Europe as co-conspirators of the United States. Sometimes they are unwilling co-conspirators. Fadlallah expressed this succinctly when he declared that "Europe has followed the United States because it is subservient to the United States, not because it actually believes in its slogans."[71] But Europe is also regarded as hostile to the cause of Islam, a view that is at one with Hezbollah's concept of the essential unity of the West in its struggle against Islam. As Islam emerges as a world power and American strength declines, the United States will need to rely increasingly upon Western Europe to sustain its campaign against Islam. Therefore,

---

[70]On the deterioration of Hezbollah's ties to Fatah, see a report in *The Times* (London), April 28, 1987.

[71]Interview with Fadlallah, *al-Majallah*, October 1-7, 1986.

Western Europe has become yet another arena of struggle between Islam and "global infidelity."

For Hezbollah, France long represented the most formidable and hated of Islam's European adversaries. Hezbollah's manifesto names France as a "leader of infidelity," along with the United States and Israel, and lists France as one of Hezbollah's "basic enemies," the only European state to earn such a distinction.[72] A preoccupation with France comes naturally to Hezbollah. When Lebanon first experienced the cultural power of the West, it was French power. When Islam's sway over Lebanon ended in this century, it was supplanted by French rule. Shaykh Subhi al-Tufayli recalled the role of France in "attacking" Lebanon in 1860, and its alleged attempt to impose Christian hegemony upon the Muslims of Lebanon.[73]

Despite waning French power in the world, Hezbollah has frequently confronted France in Lebanon. France supplied a contingent to the ill-fated Multinational Force, and at one time provided the bulk of forces for UNIFIL, the United Nations peace-keeping force in south Lebanon. France also continues to play an active role elsewhere in the Middle East, especially in providing arms and technology to Iran's enemies.

Whenever French policy is opposed by Iran or coordinated with American policy in the Middle East, France looms large in the minds of Hezbollah. Those who planned the October 1983 suicide attack against the U.S. contingent in the Multinational Force also thought it essential to strike the French contingent in an identical manner. A simultaneous campaign of kidnapping and assassination targeted French diplomats and nationals in Lebanon. The fighters of the Islamic Resistance in south Lebanon, viewing UNIFIL as an obstacle to the *jihad* against Israel, launched attacks upon the French contingent. In its war with France, Hezbollah actually brought the conflict to the enemy's territory, conducting a

---

[72]*Nass al-risala al-maftuha*, p.14.

[73]Interview with Shaykh Subhi al-Tufayli, *al-Ahd*, July 24, 1987.

bombing campaign in the French capital, with the probable assistance of Iranian officials.

Until recently, Hezbollah consistently denounced France as a party to a larger U.S.-conceived scheme to thwart Islamic revolution. "Many people think that France is behaving as if it were implementing U.S. policy in the region and that it has lost its independence in foreign policy," said Fadlallah. "That is why France is paying the price for the U.S. policy. . . . De Gaulle's France was not the same as today's France, which is more America's France."[74] The France of President François Mitterrand, maintained Fadlallah, was "acting as a broker of American policy in the Middle East."[75]

As France began to buckle under the combined pressure of Iran and Hezbollah, some of Hezbollah's spokesmen determined that France could be usefully distinguished from the United States. In Fadlallah's nuanced view, France demonstrated its independence by pursuing an opening to Iran and an initiative for the release of French hostages. According to Fadlallah, the conflict between France and the Islamic revolution was not as intractable as the conflict with the United States. Fadlallah therefore hailed former French Prime Minister Jacques Chirac's "policy of solving outstanding issues between Iran and France," a course which "represents a return to France's realistic policy of striving not to lose its economic interests in Iran or to undermine its position in the countries adjacent to it." In praise of the French, Fadlallah even opined that "the Frenchman's mentality is nearer to the Middle Eastern mentality" than the American one. "We find that the French people differ from the American people in their view of foreign policy," and so "the question of the American hostages is not politically the same as the question of the French hostages."[76]

---

[74]Interview with Fadlallah, *Le Quotidien de Paris*, September 23, 1986.

[75]Interview with Fadlallah, *Politique Internationale* (Paris), Autumn 1985.

[76]Interview with Fadlallah, *al-Nahar al-arabi wal-duwali*, July 21-27, 1986.

Husayn al-Musawi also credited French policy with some independence, although he did not forgive them for all of their past transgressions. The French acted in tandem with the United States in "helping the Phalangists and Israelis—our enemies—against the Muslims. They evacuated the Palestinians to enable the Israelis to enter Beirut." Then the French, by their participation in UNIFIL, hampered the Islamic Resistance while giving the Israelis a free hand in south Lebanon.[77]

But Musawi believed that the French were capable of acting differently, and he praised Chirac for "trying to improve relations with the Islamic Republic of Iran. The French who are helping Chirac to improve these relations are right. The French must think carefully about their future. The future does not lie with Saddam Husayn or Israel. One day the Middle East will be in Muslim hands. If France takes a step toward Islam, we will take two steps toward France," he said.[78] "The French should side with the innocent Palestinians, Lebanese, Iranians and Muslims all over the world. . . . We want to be friends with the French; we shall never hate the French."[79] These views conveyed an awareness that France might have its own interests in the Middle East, distinct from those of the United States, and that a concerted effort at intimidation could bring these differences into political play.

This was the carrot; other spokesmen of Hezbollah brandished the stick. "France now is a major colonialist power," asserted Ibrahim al-Amin. "In our view, France and the United States are the biggest exporters of terrorism in the world. They are among the countries that have created a sense of injustice among the peoples of the area. It can be said that France's policy is responsible for all that is happening,

---

[77]Interview with Husayn al-Musawi, *Le Figaro*, September 12, 1986.

[78]Interview with Husayn al-Musawi, *Le Figaro*, September 12, 1986.

[79]Interview with Husayn al-Musawi, Radio Paris, July 5, 1985, in FBIS/ME, July 8, 1985.

including what is befalling the French people."[80] In marked contrast to Fadlallah's nuanced formulations, Hezbollah's spokesmen ritually invoked France in the same breath as the United States and Israel. Ibrahim al-Amin expressly included France, along with the United States and Israel, as a state against which the Muslims must wage "open war."[81] At the height of the "war of embassies" between France and Iran in the summer of 1987, Presidents Mitterrand and Reagan were burned in effigy in demonstrations at Baalbek.[82]

Hezbollah's intimidating tactics have had an obvious effect on French policy, as France has gone to great lengths to put itself outside the circle of Hezbollah's animosity. In Lebanon, France withdrew its UNIFIL contingent from south Lebanon— one that had suffered many casualties in attacks by the Hezbollah-backed Islamic Resistance. Late in 1985, France refused to act on an American request to arrest a Hezbollah security official, 'Imad Mughniyya, who was traveling through France. Mughniyya is the man at the center of Hezbollah's hostage-taking strategy, and is wanted by the United States for his involvement in the 1985 TWA hijacking. France apparently feared complications.[83] In agreements concluded in late 1987 and early 1988 for the release of French hostages held by the Revolutionary Justice Organization and Islamic Jihad, France made far-reaching concessions.[84] It began to repay a debt owed to Iran, expelled Iranian émigrés operating against Iran from French soil and allowed the departure of people suspected of complicity in terrorism on French soil. This culminated in the restoration of France's diplomatic relations with Iran in June 1988.

---

[80]Interview with Ibrahim al-Amin, *al-Majallah*, March 19-25, 1986.

[81]Ibrahim al-Amin quoted by UPI, June 30, 1987.

[82]Photograph in *al-Ahd*, July 24, 1987.

[83]See *The New York Times*, March 14, 1986.

[84]Account of negotiations, *The International Herald Tribune*, May 9, 1988.

Hezbollah's release of all French hostages was more than an end to three cruel years of captivity. It also brought a reprieve for France by Hezbollah's spokesmen. But this reprieve was conditioned on France's conduct in Lebanon and the region. Another test loomed in mid-1989 when Lebanon's Muslim forces—including Hezbollah—lent their support to a Syrian-directed assault against the Maronite Christian heartland, for which France felt a moral and historical obligation. When French warships appeared off Lebanon's coast in August 1989, Hezbollah denounced the move as "part of the arrogant campaign aimed at taming the Muslims."[85] France's old nemesis, the so-called Revolutionary Justice Organization, also traced France's moves to U.S. instigation, and threatened the lives of American hostages: "America must know that any foolishness which the French fleet may commit will expose the hostages to danger." To bring the message home, the group threatened to "strike deep into French territory itself."[86] By its controversial deal with Iran, France had bought itself no more than a respite. Even if France sought only to fulfill its traditional role in Lebanon, it was bound to clash with Hezbollah.

Another occasional target of Hezbollah has been West Germany, a country that Hezbollah has regarded as a potential gateway to the Middle East and the rest of Europe. It was not enough that West Germany tilted toward Iran in the Gulf War and maintained an open channel to high Iranian officials. It was expected to acquiesce in the use of its territory for the war against "global infidelity."

In January 1987, West German authorities arrested a Lebanese member of Hezbollah for attempting to smuggle explosives into the country. He had been indicted for murder and hijacking in the United States for his roles in the June 1985 TWA hijacking and the murder of an American passenger. The United States formally requested his extradition. To forestall this and win his release, Hezbollah

---

[85] *The Washington Post*, August 20, 1989.

[86] *The New York Times*, August 21, 1989.

sanctioned the kidnapping in Beirut of two West Germans. Husayn al-Musawi justified the deed as a legitimate attempt to prevent any extradition and secure the release of the accused.[87] In June 1987, West Germany decided not to extradite the suspect to the United States but to try him in West Germany; the West German hostages were subsequently released. The trial resulted in a life sentence for the hijacker and another wave of threats by Hezbollah against West Germany, including the kidnapping of two West German relief workers.

West Germany's conduct earned it a place in Hezbollah's discourse against the West. Its stand against abuse of its hospitality was explained by its subservience to the United States and its moral servitude to Israel. Fadlallah appealed to West Germans as kindred victims, who should understand better than others how "the Americans and Israelis want to rob us of our free will." The German people, "through no fault of their own," were "victims of history and of the policy of the superpowers. As a result, the German people have been divided and cannot develop as an independent political force." At the same time, the Israelis burdened the Germans with a "complex of eternal guilt," when in fact "the average German also suffered under Hitler's yoke."[88] The demand that West Germany free itself from the grip of the United States was echoed by Husayn al-Musawi: "We like and respect the Germans very much, but their government is too weak vis-à-vis the Americans. They should adopt a more independent stance," and cease acting like a "United States colony."[89]

Hezbollah's intimidation of West Germany constituted an extreme example of its refusal to accord neutrality to any country in the battle between "infidelity and faith." West Germany had done nothing to provoke Iran, and played no

---

[87]Musawi interview, Hamburg DPA, February 4, 1987, in FBIS/ME, February 5, 1987.

[88]Fadlallah interview, *Der Spiegel*, April 1, 1985.

[89]Musawi interview, Hamburg DPA, February 4, 1987, in FBIS/ME, February 5, 1987.

role in confronting Hezbollah in Lebanon. It had acted in a manner consonant with a basic respect for international law, arresting a man wanted by the United States for an act defined in international law as terror. But at that moment in time, Hezbollah's struggle required a European free zone where arrest was unlikely or carried no penalty. West Germany's denial of that zone was understood not as neutrality but as complicity.

Great Britain also occupies a place in the imagination of Hezbollah. The role of Britain in the subjugation of Iran and its contribution to the establishment of Zionism in Palestine have been perceived as examples of Britain's complicity in the wider conspiracy against Islam. But Britain did not figure high on the list of Hezbollah's priorities in its first years of growth, because that list was long. Unlike the United States and France, Great Britain did not take part in the Multinational Force and generally maintained a low profile in Lebanon. Britain did not warrant mention in Hezbollah's manifesto and its flags were not burned at Hezbollah's rallies. Anglican Church envoy Terry Waite even volunteered to be a mediator between Hezbollah and the United States, as though his nationality and standing established his neutrality in the eyes of Hezbollah.

Waite's kidnapping in January 1987, constituted the ultimate rejection by Hezbollah of all such claims to neutrality. It did not matter that Waite was British and that Britain had stayed clear of the conflict in Lebanon. Nor did it matter that he operated under the humanitarian auspices of the Archbishop of Canterbury. Those responsible for Waite's kidnapping had no difficulty in reducing him from his self-proclaimed status as disinterested mediator to that of one more conspirator whose only business in Lebanon was plotting with the United States against Islam. The resolution of the Waite kidnapping and the release of two other British hostages became dependent on a series of British political and economic concessions to Iran. Following the Rushdie affair, Britain briefly displaced France in Hezbollah's imagination as the European power in closest collusion with the United States and Israel. The British flag was burned at Hezbollah rallies and

British policy was denounced as having been hostile to Islam from time immemorial.[90]

There is obviously a core of truth in Hezbollah's linking of the United States with France, West Germany and Britain. They share cultural legacies, values and interests that buttress Hezbollah's understanding of the West as a counter to Islam. A powerful West was fashioned by an omnipotent God to test the faith of Muslims and to separate true believers from hypocrites and doubters. This challenge has taken the form of a conspiracy to corrupt Islam. The West European democracies, which have been corrupted by the vast power of America, are the willing or unwilling co-conspirators of the United States. When France sends forces to Lebanon and sells arms to Iraq, when West Germany condemns Hezbollah's most devoted soldiers to prison, when Britain offers refuge to a Muslim apostate whose book undermines the very foundations of Islam, they are doing the bidding of America. Hostage-holding is partly intended to weaken the hold of the United States on its co-conspirators. There are no "Western" hostages, but hostages from individual Western countries, whose release is predicated upon steps of withdrawal from the conspiracy against Islam.

## SOVIET UNION: "NO BETTER THAN THE AMERICANS"

Hezbollah has systematically denounced Soviet long-term intentions in the Middle East. Its objective, said Fadlallah on one occasion, is "to gain access to the Mediterranean and to impose their control on the area's oil and natural resources. Although the Soviet Union claims to want to help the people of the Middle East achieve their freedom, we know for a fact that for a long time now it has drifted away from the Communist ideal of popular liberations. It now acts as a superpower, as one can observe in Afghanistan."[91] But while Hezbollah's

---

[90]Account of Hezbollah's anti-Rushdie demonstrations in Beirut and Baalbek, *al-Ahd*, March 3, 1989.

[91]Interview with Fadlallah, *Politique internationale*, Autumn 1985.

manifesto of 1985 denounced the Soviet invasion of Afghanistan, Soviet intervention in Iran and Soviet support for Iraq, it also determined that "in Lebanon and in the region of Palestine, we are mainly concerned with confronting America, because it has the greatest influence among the countries of world arrogance, and also with confronting Israel, the ulcerous growth of world Zionism."[92]

On that account, the movement's discourse against "global infidelity" tends to sidestep the Soviet Union. The strategy of avoidance found its greatest expression in 1985, when a splinter group of a Hezbollah-backed Sunni fundamentalist movement in Tripoli kidnapped four Soviet diplomats in Beirut, killing one before releasing the rest. Hezbollah's spokesmen took a uniformly firm position against the kidnapping. As Husayn al-Musawi explained:

> We all know the ideological conflict between Communism and Islam. . . . But our view is that dealing with the Soviets in the manner they were dealt with in Beirut was quite inappropriate. We as Muslims should stick to our priorities in the conflict. Our conflict is with Israel and should be confined to Israel. It is wrong to widen the circle of conflict to involve the parties which we do not wish to call friends of the Arabs or Muslims, or widen it in such a way not in keeping with the priorities of the conflict with Israel. Muslims should think on this basis, and the kidnapping of the Soviets in my view is wrong.[93]

Subhi al-Tufayli also said that the kidnapping ran counter to Islamic interests: "This is not because the Soviets are supporting the Muslims; they basically support the existence of Israel and ensure its security. However, we believe that the Muslims will not benefit from detaining or killing the Soviets. . . . We take

---

[92]See "Nass al-risala al-maftuha," p.27.

[93]Interview with Husayn al-Musawi, *al-Nahar al-arabi wal-duwali*, October 28-November 3, 1985.

this position because the kidnapping does not promote our confrontation with Israel and might perhaps have the opposite effect."[94]

Therefore, Hezbollah did not sanction an active campaign against the Soviet Union. But recently, Hezbollah's spokesmen have devoted more attention to evidence of Soviet complicity in the wider conspiracy against Islam, especially the growing accord between the United States and the Soviet Union on regional issues. As Subhi al-Tufayli commented on one of the Reagan-Gorbachev summits: "What happens in these summits is that the two superpowers determine their interests through games, acts of sedition and wars which they provoke here and there, so that they may keep control, on the one hand, and maintain the balance of interests between them on the other. The result of this summit is likely to be that the oppressed will fall victim to wars in which they give their lives and blood for the sake of the two superpowers and their allies."[95] Hezbollah's dualistic vision of the world can accommodate only one fundamental division of humankind, and the Soviet Union has fallen under suspicion for collaboration with the United States against the interests of Islam.

The Soviet Union's position on the Gulf War also evoked threats from Hezbollah. Hezbollah's spokesmen roundly denounced the Soviet offer to protect Kuwaiti ships, which preceded the American reflagging in the summer of 1987.[96] In March 1988, Hezbollah called for an anti-Soviet demonstration in Beirut, following reports that Iraq had used Soviet-supplied missiles to attack Tehran. The demonstration, which would have been the first by Hezbollah against the Soviet Union, was cancelled only at the last minute, in deference to an Iranian decision.[97] Demonstrations did occur in Iran.

---

[94]Interview with Subhi al-Tufayli, *as-Safir*, October 24, 1985.

[95]Interview with Subhi al-Tufayli, *al-Ahd*, July 24, 1987.

[96]Interview with Subhi al-Tufayli, *al-Nahar al-arabi wal-duwali*, December 21-27, 1987.

[97]Voice of Islam (clandestine), March 11, 1988, announcing cancellation of the demonstration.

Far more sinister for Hezbollah have been signs of Soviet readiness to contribute to an Arab-Israeli peace process. The emerging Soviet-Israeli dialogue and Soviet support for an international conference are interpreted by Hezbollah as evidence of an increasingly hostile attitude of the Soviet Union toward Islam. "At a moment when Muslims are opening their eye to the American political dangers in the region," says Husayn al-Musawi, "they should also open their other eye to the dangerous campaigns against Muslim interests which the Soviet moves represent." The headline of an article on Soviet policy in Hezbollah's weekly newspaper declared that, "They Are No Better Than the Americans."[98] In Hezbollah's vision, a Soviet-American effort to legitimize Israel and freeze the present distribution of power in the region would constitute a massive obstacle to the emergence of Islam as a world power and Islam's redrawing of the regional map.

---

[98]See *al-Ahd*, May 5, 1987.

# V   CONCLUSION: THE CONTINUING JIHAD

An essential part of Hezbollah's vision is the dichotomy between Islam and infidelity. This dichotomy is a representation of the world as it is supposed to be, not as it is, and there have been voices within Hezbollah and Iran that have urged a distinction between fundamental principle and day-to-day practice. Fadlallah, for one, has made this argument in many subtle ways, by affirming the possibility of a balanced relationship with the West and urging more subtle exploitation of the internal dichotomies of the West. But his influence has been inconsistent, for without an insistence on the fundamental dichotomy between Islam and infidelity, Hezbollah stands to lose its moral compass. At issue is the truth of Islam. If Islam is truth, then to advocate the coexistence of truth and falsehood—of Islam and those who negate it—is to advocate corruption. Even the Prophet Muhammad had to retreat on occasion, and he employed ruses in diplomacy and war, but his spirit remained pure. *The Satanic Verses* was a plot to legitimize contemporary corruption by asserting that even the Prophet Muhammad, when faced with a pressing exigency, could not resist the temptation to tamper with God's revelation.

The remarkable outburst against Rushdie for portraying the prophet as a pragmatist was a reaction against those who affirmed that the Islamic revolution in Iran had substituted *realpolitik* for revelation. Western speculation about pragmatism, realism and moderation has been understood by many in Iran and Hezbollah as an attempt to corrupt. Because Iran and Hezbollah overhear Western predictions of their impending corruption, these analyses sometimes function as self-defeating prophecies.

In Hezbollah, as in Iran, there are many who fiercely resist the notion that corruption is inevitable. For them, the continuing struggle against "global infidelity" is nothing less than a theological necessity that establishes the truth of Islam. The *jihad* defines Islam and distinguishes between the pure faith of Hezbollah—the "Party of God"—and the compromised faith of backsliding Muslims. The reality of a conspiracy of falsehood to corrupt Islam is so crucial to Hezbollah's understanding of Islamic truth that no contemporary event is subject to interpretation outside of its context. This conception of politics is fundamentally dualistic, pitting absolute good against absolute evil in a zero-sum game. Virtue is the demonstrated willingness to suffer martyrdom for truth.

In the case of Lebanon's Hezbollah, the existence of a global struggle is more than a theological necessity. It clearly serves a number of specifically Lebanese Shi'ite needs. Through their membership in Hezbollah, the clerics and the movement's rank-and-file adherents seek to escape narrow allegiances and embrace a vast cause that transcends the boundaries of family, clan, sect and state. Through one's affiliation with Hezbollah, the individual ceases to be a Lebanese Shi'ite Arab—a member of a disadvantaged sect in a small war-torn state. Through Hezbollah the individual becomes a Muslim, a member of a religious-political community spanning three continents. The adherent of Hezbollah becomes a participant in a world movement founded by the Imam Khomeini that is devoted to redressing the imbalance between Islam and infidelity. It is this exalting sense of belonging that constitutes the secret of Hezbollah's strength.

Hezbollah's struggle, says an editorial in the movement's newspaper, "is an inseparable part of the overall Islamic strategy in the great and comprehensive confrontation with the aggression of Zionists, Crusaders and world arrogance." Hezbollah is a "forward position" of this struggle, which is being conducted simultaneously on many fronts.[1] This is a mission above human history, a task of essentially eschatological significance. A sense of divine purpose accounts for Hezbollah's appeal and constitutes the essence of its vision— a vision as vast in its conception as Lebanon is small.

Hezbollah has never confused its strategy and tactics with that vision. The former are subject to constant reassessment due to changing circumstances, always with a mind toward the conservation of force. Violence is only used when the threat of violence fails, and Hezbollah only threatens violence when it fails to persuade. But Hezbollah's vision remains the fixed beacon to which all possible strategies and tactics ultimately lead. The concept of struggle with the forces of "global infidelity" remains a permanent theme in Hezbollah's dominant discourse, although that struggle may advance in fits and starts. It is difficult for a movement with Hezbollah's limited resources to struggle simultaneously against all the forces of "global infidelity." When appeased or temporarily deterred by any one of its opponents, Hezbollah reorders its priorities and shifts resources against another opponent. But such shifts are not opportunities for final reconciliation. They are always understood and justified in terms of the larger vision and are subject to constant reappraisal. "We desire peace," says Husayn al-Musawi, "but not a peace that means slavery. Sometimes we can compromise, as for example in the war with Iraq, but our principled positions do not change."[2]

The apparent end of the Gulf War, the dramatic shifts in Iran's internal power balance, Syria's continuing drive to consolidate its position in Lebanon and the outbreak of the *intifadah* have inspired several reappraisals. Hezbollah is now under many contradictory pressures, and the responses of its ideologues and strategists have varied.

There are those in the movement who favor suspending Hezbollah's active campaign against the West in order to channel more resources into escalation of the struggle against

---

[1] Unsigned article in *al-Ahd*, March 7, 1986.

[2] Interview with Husayn al-Musawi, *Nouveau Magazine*, July 23, 1988.

Israel and Hezbollah's Lebanese adversaries. Others believe that Hezbollah must maintain some level of activity, real and symbolic, on all fronts of confrontation with "global infidelity." The former suggest that at least some of the foreign hostages be released, on the assumption that they are a depreciating asset. The latter insist that those who have been taken not be released, since this would be widely interpreted as a sign of flagging zeal, unless done on the basis of a complete capitulation to terms dictated by the interests of Islam. Yet these differences have not split the movement, for the internal debate is conducted in the narrow doctrinal categories of Hezbollah's millenarian vision.

The combination of millenarian belief, charismatic leadership and Shi'ite stoicism in the face of adversity make it difficult to determine the conditions under which Hezbollah might lose heart and accept the world as it is—a world in which "global infidelity" commands many times the power of combined Islam. There have been comparable movements in the modern history of Islam, but they offer contradictory precedents. Some grew to accept the power of nonbelievers as one of God's mysteries and learned to live within its constraints. Others resisted and went down in defeat, preferring martyrdom to corruption. But even those movements that reached a compromise with the West did not do so until they had experienced numerous disappointments and had committed their full intellectual resources to reformulating their vision. That painful process was punctuated by attempts to reassert the original vision, lest it be corrupted beyond recognition.

There are signs that some in Hezbollah may have begun to rethink not only the movement's strategy but its premises. Second thoughts have been inspired by experiences which have demonstrated just how wide the gap between vision and reality has become. Other Muslim movements, faced with the overwhelming power of the West, were led to reinterpret the concept of *jihad* as a form of peaceful struggle over minds and hearts. If Hezbollah ever reaches this point, it will be due to the resolve shown by its adversaries. A past lack of resolve, rooted in a fear of provoking Hezbollah and a desire to appease it, only strengthened the hand of those in the movement who wished to push harder and faster for the achievement of millenarian goals. The setbacks dealt to the cause of revolutionary Islam—in the Gulf, on Hezbollah's line of confrontation with Israel, in Western courtrooms—have compelled those responsible for guiding Iran and Hezbollah to search their souls. But that rethinking is by no means complete. Until a lengthy process of disillusionment and reformulation is brought to its conclusion, Hezbollah will conduct its *jihad* by both persuasion and force, testing its resolve and unity against those of the West.

# POLICY PAPERS SERIES

*Editors:*
**Martin Indyk**
**John Hannah**

**Policy Papers may be purchased for $9.95 from The Washington Institute,**
**50 F Street, N.W., Suite 8800, Washington, D.C., 20001, (202) 783-0226.**